Beaver

Animal

Series editor: Jonathan Burt

Beaver

Rachel Poliquin

REAKTION BOOKS

Published by
REAKTION BOOKS LTD
33 Great Sutton Street
London EC1V 0DX, UK
www.reaktionbooks.co.uk

First published 2015
Copyright © Rachel Poliquin 2015

Printed and bound in China by 1010 Printing International Ltd

A catalogue record for this book is available from the British Library

ISBN 978 1 78023 423 6

Contents

Introduction

The Beaver itself is not easily seen, being nocturnal and
secretive, but it can be spotted in ponds, lakes, or large
streams at twilight by a quiet observer.
'Castor canadensis, American Beaver', *Encyclopedia of Life*,
www.eol.org

It is hard to see a beaver. For a large animal which boldly makes
its presence known with gnawed stumps and massive engineering
projects, a beaver is surprisingly difficult to spot. Gliding through
the water at dusk with just its eyes, nose and ears above surface,
a beaver can see, smell and hear you, but you will likely miss it
altogether.

And then, it is difficult to know which beaver to see. There
is always more than one. The beaver's journey within human
cultures has been a journey of beaver pieces and parts. At various
historical moments the beaver has been synonymous with its
testicles, musk, asceticism, fur, architectural prowess, collectiv-
ism, industry, animal instinct, environmental engineering and
a few things more besides. When Samuel Pepys wrote in his diary
on 27 June 1661, 'This day Mr Holden sent me a bever, which cost
me 4*l* 5*s*', he meant Mr Holden sent him a felted beaver hat.[1]
When Thomas Carlyle weighed the merits of a 'beaver intellect'
in his *Latter-Day Pamphlets* (1850) he used 'beaver' to describe
the unheroic mentality of an honest yet plodding worker. More
recently, environmental groups who champion the reintroduction of beavers into American lakes and rivers are self-described
as 'beaver believers'. It is not that beaver believers have faith in the
animals' ability to re-establish themselves in their native habitats.
Rather, 'beaver' is shorthand for the ecological transformation

beavers accomplish by simply living their lives. Beaver believers believe that beavers, by managing water levels and creating wetland habitats, will mitigate the worst effects of a changing climate. Saying 'beaver' (or rather *castor*, to use the Latin) to a Renaissance physician would have produced a small vial of musky effluence from a beaver's scent organs. Saying 'beaver' in the twenty-first century can prove far more risqué since the word has become sexual slang for female genitalia. Seeing a beaver means seeing the right beaver, and saying 'beaver' always requires an explanation of which beaver is intended.

Evidence a beaver has been hard at work.

More basically, it is exceedingly hard to see a creature that no longer exists. Simply put, the beaver's history is a long tale of systematic eradication. For an animal that has become intimately associated with busyness, the beaver has been notorious for its absences.

The bison is perhaps the most iconic of the North American animals almost hunted into oblivion. From the 50 million that once roamed the great plains of North America, only a thousand remained in 1889. But the beaver – although smaller, quieter and less romantic for big sky dreamers – was the even more significant animal in North America's early history. Beavers were the motivating cause for North America's first colonies, and the quest for a steady supply of beaver skins was one of the main drivers of expansion towards the Pacific coast. As eastern forests and wetlands were stripped clean, traders were drawn further and further westwards in the pursuit of the lucrative fur. No one knows how many beavers once populated North America. They likely numbered in the tens of millions and occupied most bodies of water from northern Canada to northern Mexico. But by 1812, Thomas Douglas Selkirk, part owner of the Hudson's Bay Company, the largest fur-trading monopoly the world has ever seen, was forced to admit that 'Beavers, formerly so numerous, are rapidly approaching to the point of complete extermination.'[2]

But the beaver stands apart from other stories of species endangerment and loss. While there is much to lament in the devastation of millions of beavers, the damage was not without significant ecological benefit: the near eradication of the North American beaver likely saved another beaver on the other side of the Atlantic. There are in fact two beavers – the North American

Illustration of a beaver skeleton from Georges-Louis Leclerc, Comte de Buffon, *Histoire naturelle* (1760).

beaver (*Castor canadensis*) and the Eurasian beaver (*Castor fiber*). Separated millions of years ago, the two nevertheless share a conjoined history of disappearing.

Beavers once roamed Eurasia from Wales to eastern Siberia and from the Turkish coast of the Black Sea to the northernmost tip of Scandinavia. But Eurasian beavers rapidly receded from the early Middle Ages onwards, as if by an eastwardly ebbing tide. They were killed for the fabled medicinal properties of their musk. Their fish-like tails were eaten by the piously abstemious during Lenten fasts. They were hunted for their fur until there was hardly a beaver left. And then, just as beavers were tottering on the very brink of extinction, an unknown continent teeming with beavers was discovered to the west, and the second continental wave of beaver eradication was set in motion.

Beavers pervade the mythologies of North America's first Nations. The Haida of the northwest coast of British Columbia tell how Raven stole salmon from the Beaver people by rolling up their stream like a carpet. The river was so heavy that Raven was forced to rest on treetops as he flew home. The Beaver people tried to stop him by gnawing down the trees. As each tree fell and Raven wearily set flight again, a few salmon spilt out to form the great salmon rivers of British Columbia. The Tlingit Nation, also of the Pacific Northwest, has a myth about a porcupine who stole the provisions a beaver laid up for winter. As punishment the beavers swam the porcupine to an island and left him there to die. But as soon as the north wind blew, the channel froze and the porcupine escaped back to his people to plot revenge on the beaver. The porcupine and his people carried the beaver to the top of a tree, thinking he would be stranded and perish. But the beaver ate the tree from the top down. And the Cree Nation of the Great Plains tells a story about the trickster Wisagatcak

A beaver mask from the Kwakwaka'wakw nation of the Pacific Northwest.

who tried to kill the Great Beaver. Just as Wisagatcak was about to throw his spear, the Great Beaver cast a spell on a muskrat, causing it to bite Wisagatcak on the rump. Angry and sore, Wisagatcak hacked apart the beaver's lodge and dam, but the Great Beaver was more powerful. Instead of running through the broken dam, the waters rose and continued to rise until the entire world was flooded.

Although they tell very different stories, the myths all seem to have emerged from living alongside beavers. Supernatural beavers are not so very different from the flesh and blood animals. All beavers manage river systems, store up food for winter and chew down trees faster than their foes thought possible. In a sense, the beavers of North American myths are easy to see. They are creative, industrious, accomplished creatures with an integrated set of skills and talents.

In contrast, most western myths arose from not knowing beavers, which partially explains why writers tore beavers into succulent titbits and philosophical dainties. Stretching back to Aesop's fables and Herodotus' histories, strange and improbable

It is hard to see a beaver, even when one is nearby.

tales have been spun around the beaver. Although the stories were all inspired by the beaver's genuinely exceptional features – its powerful teeth, unique fishy tail, pungent scent and architectural prowess – the fables and half-truths have almost nothing to do with the living animals. In the myth-makers' defence, the beaver's anatomical parts and talents are altogether worthy of the wild fictions and intellectual infatuations. If beavers had gone extinct long ago, their genuine endowments would read like medieval fancy to modern readers. But beavers survived, which is perhaps the most remarkable beaver tale of all.

After an introductory dissection of beaver biology and its cultural and evolutionary history, the following chapters explore four very different romances with four exceptional beaver parts: beaver musk, beaver fur, beaver architecture and beaver ecological management. The romances have nothing in common with each other except that they all cast beavers as good and worthy beasts. Beavers' attitudes towards their musky testicles was a lesson in virtue. Their fur was an economic boon. Their architectural skills were parables of human industry and co-operation, and their ability to create wetland habitats has elevated beavers into ecological warriors. Only in recent decades, as beaver populations rebound with astonishing vigour across the northern hemisphere and into the southern hemisphere, have beavers been seen as anything less than good.

The cultural history of the beaver is a story of excesses and absences, parts and pieces, misinformation, fables and triumphs. It is a tale of how humans have broken beavers into lucrative pieces and recombined them into philosophical assertions. But whether humans have ingested beaver musk, worn beaver fur, admired the animal's industry, or heralded the world's second largest rodent as a climate change hero, at the centre of it all is the busy body of the biological beaver. And that is where we begin.

1 Beaver

The beaver still appears to be encountered, seldom or never plentifully, always in greatly diminished numbers, and generally with an extreme and constantly increasing rarity.
Charles Wilson, *Notes on the Prior Existence of Castor fiber in Scotland, with its Ancient and Present Distribution in Europe, and on the Use of Castoreum* (1858)

Sir Hans Sloane, the great eighteenth-century collector, naturalist and physician, kept a young female beaver in his Bloomsbury garden in the middle of London. She was a paunch-bellied beast and only half grown, measuring 30 in. (76 cm) from the tip of her nose to the end of her tail. She lived mainly on bread, which she held with both paws, sitting on her haunches like a squirrel. Occasionally she nibbled the willow boughs that were brought for her, but she preferred the vines growing in Sloane's garden and gnawed several of them down to the roots. She was never heard to make any noise except a few short grunts when chased or angered. Most of all she loved to swim in a fountain filled with flounders.

Where the beaver hailed from is lost to time, but considering the exotic origins of Sloane's other garden beasts (a red-headed crane from Bengal, a blind Arctic fox from Greenland and a large greenish lizard from Malaga), she was likely captured in the New World, probably from the region around the Saint Laurence River as it flows out to the Atlantic Ocean. Also unknown is when the beaver arrived in Sloane's garden, but she was decidedly dead three months later when Cromwell Mortimer, Sloane's neighbour, good friend and fellow physician, dissected her remains in 1733. The beaver had suffered a bout of convulsive fits but had recovered and was well enough until the day she was torn apart by a dog.

Der Biber. Castor Fiber. Lin.

An endearingly podgy beaver from Johann Matthäus Bechstein's *Getreue Abbildungen Naturhistorischer Gegenstände*, 1795.

Nothing much was left of the beaver after the attack, but Mortimer was determined to dissect her remains and publish his findings in one of the leading scientific journals of the day. 'She was so torn', he writes in *Philosophical Transactions*, 'that we could see nothing Particular in the Heart, or in the Lungs. In the *Abdomen* the Liver and Kidnies were quite torn a-pieces. There were several Holes bit through the Stomach.' Luckily for Mortimer, the beaver's back end and most particularly her 'Parts of Generation' were sufficiently unharmed for him to observe the exact size, shape and location of her uterus, ovaries, bladder, scent organs, vagina, anus and single posterior opening, or cloaca, which Mortimer calls the 'great *fissure*'.[1]

That the torn body of a female beaver could offer anything of interest to the learned world of eighteenth-century natural science suggests just how unexplored beaver biology was. Yet beavers were hardly new or strangely exotic. Mortimer himself likely owned a beaver hat and may have prescribed beaver musk for his sickly patients. The problem was not that beavers were unknown in Europe but rather that they had been known for centuries as animal products, not living creatures.

Beavers were already extinct in England by the twelfth century. In 1188, Gerald of Wales claimed that the last beaver colony in all of Great Britain lived on the River Teifi in southwest Wales. A few beavers may have been spotted in Scotland, 'but [were] very scarce'.[2] By the time Michael Drayton crafted his pastoral poem, *Poly-Olbion*, in 1612, no British beavers remained, not even in the River Teifi, or 'Tivy' as Drayton calls it:

> More famous long agone, than the salmon's leap,
> For beavers *Tivy* was, in her strong banks that bred,
> Which else no other brook of Britain nourished:
> Where Nature, in the shape of this now-perish'd beast
> His property did seem t'have wondrously exprest.[3]

Beavers were eradicated from Italy by the sixteenth century and were extremely rare in France by the early eighteenth, although, remarkably, a small community of 30 beavers survived on the Low Rhône, forming one of the eight populations which were used to reintroduce beavers throughout Eurasia in the twenty-first century. Vast numbers of beavers once occupied the river systems in Germany, Austria, Switzerland and Poland, but by the time Mortimer dissected his beaver, 'they are now all destroy'd'.[4]

As physical beavers withdrew eastwards across Europe, literary beavers flourished. The ancient Greek physician Hippocrates had prescribed beaver musk as a healing remedy, which ensured castoreum would be included in every pharmaceutical text until the nineteenth century. Likewise, Aesop crafted a moral tale about the beaver, which firmly established the animal within the canon of fables and perpetuated a bawdy beaver falsehood for nearly two thousand years. Beavers also make regular appearances in a variety of Renaissance and early modern texts. Dante Alighieri included a beaver in the *Divine Comedy*, and the seventeenth-century natural philosopher Athanasius Kircher confirmed that beavers were welcomed aboard Noah's ark and stationed in their own stall next to a tub of water shared with mermaids and otters.

Despite such literary abundances, the beaver's physical absence left its mark. For millennia, the standard beaver description suggests a little-known animal, unexamined and on the wane; of beaver traces, not biological beasts.

From the English *beaver*, the early French *bièvre*, the German *biber*, the Slavic roots *bobr* or *bibr*, or the Swedish prefix *bjur*, the sheer number of beaver-derived place names dotted across Europe indicates how plentiful beavers once were. In England, there is the market town of Beverley in Yorkshire and Beaver Close in Surrey. France has the towns of Fougères-sur-Bièvre, Monthou-sur-Bièvre and Bièvres. Dotted across Switzerland, Austria and Germany, like so many deserted beaver lodges, are cities named Bibra, Bibern, Biberbach ('beaver stream') and Biebrich ('rich in beavers'). Germany has a Bibra river and two Biber rivers – one running along the Germany–Switzerland border into the Rhine, the other flowing through Bavaria to the Danube. Continuing eastwards through Poland there are the towns of Bober and Bóbrka, and a Bóbr river flowing through southwest Poland and north of the Czech Republic. Ukraine has a Bibrka and Bobr. Sweden is dotted with Bjurbäcker, Bjurfors and Bjurlund.

Beavers once occupied most of the Eurasian continent. Their southern range extended through Turkey, Iran and Iraq. The ancient Persian river goddess Anahita was said to wear a robe made from the skins of 30 male beavers, and the fifth-century BC

1. le Cochon d'inde.   2. le Castor.

The average beaver is about 20 times bigger than a large guinea pig.

historian Herodotus recorded that beavers inhabited the wetlands of Pontus, an ancient Greek name for the Turkish coast of the Black Sea. To the east, beavers were found throughout China, Mongolia and Russia. Another of the eight surviving Eurasian populations, totalling about 100 beavers, lived in the Urungu River system in northwest Mongolia. Another 30–40 beavers survived in Yenisei River in the Tuva Mountains of Middle Siberia. To the north, beavers inhabited all of Scandinavia, and to the west they touched the Atlantic Ocean, although they never crossed the Irish Sea.

A Middle Eastern beaver as sketched by Engelbert Kaempfer on his tour of Persia in 1683–4.

Despite beavers' widespread presence, even the earliest descriptions seem to draw away from the living creature. Perhaps Aristotle is to blame; in his *History of Animals*, he describes beavers as flatter than otters, with strong teeth and rough fur. Pliny the Elder followed, writing that 'the tail is like that of a fish; in the other parts of the body they resemble the otter'.[5] In other words, otters and fish were the common animals; beavers were the rarity. And this became the standard descriptive formula for the next millennium and a half. Beavers were always explained by way of comparison with other, better-known creatures. Beavers were never just themselves.

Of particular interest was the beaver's amphibious character. In classical zoology, animals were understood to inhabit one of

20

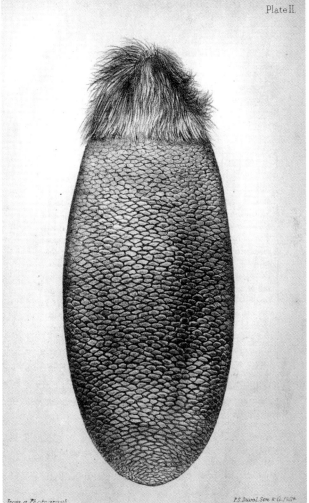

Plate II

The scale-like pattern on a beaver's tail is formed by skin-deep indentations.

From a Photograph.

P.S.Duval Son & Co. Phila

TAIL of BEAVER, ⅝ nat. Size.

three realms – birds occupied the air, beasts lived on land and fish swam in the water. A few animals blurred the boundaries to form connective links in the Chain of Being. Just as bats linked birds and beasts, beavers linked beasts to fishes. The beaver's aquatic lifestyle suggested to sixteenth-century Italian physician and naturalist Pietro Andrea Mattioli that 'the beaver is an animal with a double nature', sometimes seen on land, but most often 'living in the water with the fishes'.[6] In fact, the beaver was known to be such a bifurcated creature that the Roman Catholic Church declared it to be a fish behind and a beast in front: its tail and belly were deemed fish and so could be eaten on days of fasting including non-meat Fridays and through Lenten abstinence.[7] Beaver tail was considered a great delicacy, having the flavour – the French naturalist Pierre Belon writes – of a nicely dressed eel.[8]

Admittedly, the beaver's tail is a unique structure – no other creature has anything quite like it. A little over a foot long, half a foot wide and an inch thick (30 × 6 × 2.5 cm), the tail is bald, shaped like a large lozenge and covered with overlapping keratin scales. Platypus tails have a similar lozenge shape but are furry; muskrat tails have keratin scales but are thin like a rat's. In contrast, beaver tails really do resemble a large, flat, brown fish, and it is hardly surprising that such a tail played into the spiritual intensity of the Renaissance world view. God had not only created the world and each and every creature, fruit and seashell, but had imprinted them with signs that, if properly deciphered, would lead the faithful towards richer understanding. The visible marks on the surface of things spoke a deeper truth, and nature was a vehicle for imaginative possibilities. The brain-like shape of walnuts, for example, was a sign that the nuts eased brain fevers. The fish-like shape of a beaver's tail conferred a fishy essence to the animal for, as Bartholomaeus Anglicus wrote in 1240, beavers

A fish-tailed beaver depicted alongside the purifying powers of a unicorn's horn.

The tusked boar-beaver of Biberach; taken from a 15th-century heraldic illustration.

A regal wolf-beaver from Ulrich Rösch's 15th-century book of heraldry, the *Haggenberg Codex*.

must keep their tails wet as 'the tayll is of fishy kynde, he may not without water be long kepte without corruption'.[9]

The beaver's fishiness was augmented by the animal's supposed pescatarian diet. The great eighteenth-century naturalist Georges-Louis Leclerc, Comte de Buffon, went so far as to claim that the beaver's tail was a sort of fishy excrescence. As Buffon explained, animals which live on one kind of food will in time undergo 'a kind of transformation', whereby 'the nourishment no longer assimilates entirely to the form of the animal, but the animal assimilates in part to the form of the nourishment'.[10] By eating so much fish, the beaver was turned partly into a fish. The truth of the matter is that beavers are strict vegetarians; they prefer the underbark of aspens, cottonwood and willow trees and also eat various pond weeds and water lilies.

The fish-tailed beaver was only one of many ancient beaver distortions. Concurrent traditions saw the animal quite differently. The coat of arms of Biberach, for example, depicts a stocky pig

24

with a tufted tail and the upward-thrusting tusks of a boar, described in heraldry as 'armed gules'. The beaver in the armorial for Ulrich Rösch, abbot of Saint Gall, was wolfishly lean but also sported dagger-like tusks. Why tusks? Perhaps they endowed the retiring beaver with a visual fierceness. Or perhaps the tusks arose from exaggerated tales of beavers' prominent teeth and tree-cutting ability. Endowed with 5 cm- (2 in.)-long orange incisors, beavers can snap a sapling in a bite or two and fell trees over a metre in diameter in a few nights' work. Moreover, both Aristotle and Pliny claimed beavers had a bone-breaking bite. According to Pliny, 'the bite of this animal is terrible'. If beavers 'seize a man by any part of his body, they will never loose their hold until his bones are broken and crackle under their teeth'.[11] (An unfortunate side note: in 2013 a beaver attacked a man in Belarus, biting him in the thigh. The bite severed an artery and the man bled to death in 30 minutes. Not Pliny's bone-crushing bite, but devastating nonetheless.)

Although most heraldic beavers were far from fishy, the beaver's aquatic nature lurked in a few representations. In his book of heraldry from 1611, John Guillim classified the beaver among 'Creatures of exorbitant kinde' due to its amphibious nature.[12] This might explain the zoologically cryptic sea-dog, a biologically mismatched creature with scales, fangs, clawed webbed feet and a broad scaly tail like a beaver.

A rather different sort of bite characterized the beaver within fables. According to Aesop a beaver, when cornered by a hunter, will bite off his testicles to save his life. If such peculiar behaviour were not odd enough (beaver testicles were believed to contain a healing balm), medieval manuscripts often illustrated the fable with fierce blue dogs. The dog-beavers are eccentric, even by medieval standards. Perhaps the imagery can be traced back to ancient Persia, where the beaver was known as *sag-e ābī*, or aquatic

The beavers depicted with upward-thrusting tusks in a 15th-century armorial from southern Germany.

The enigmatic sea-dog, with a fish in its mouth, is endowed with a beaver's tail and the claws of a lion.

Despite its appearance, the blue animal can easily be identified as a beaver by its testicles, which have just been torn from its back-end.

dog, which might also explain the origins of the sea-dog. The ancient Greek physician Hippocrates, for example, claimed that the best castoreum came from Pontus and therefore called beavers Pontic dogs.

The beaver visions blossomed from different beaver parts – fish tails, formidable teeth and healing testicles – and existed side by side without confusion or conflict, in part because they each inhabited a different mentality. The fishy beaver biologically proved that the natural world was harmoniously knitted together by a wondrous creator: each beast was divinely appointed to its proper realm, or realms in the case of the bifurcated beaver. The tusked beaver animated a ferocious, albeit erroneous, psychological potency for symbolic human self-representation. And the self-castrating beaver was more of an allegorical beast which offered a moral directive on how to live the good life. On the one hand, the diversity of beavers is hardly unusual – most animals occupy multiple and often contradictory compartments within the human imagination. But what makes the beaver rather special is that wildly different imaginings were not inspired by beavers but by their idiosyncratic features. No animal has a tail anything like a beaver's. The beaver has scent organs which are unique in the animal world. And its teeth, while not exceptional in structure, accomplish the extraordinary. Into this mix, add one more essential ingredient – the beaver's almost-extinct status. Barely-there creatures with rare and remarkable features, beavers were perfectly built to inspire ever-more rapturous tales and biological reveries.

As physical beavers receded eastwards through Europe, a continent literally teeming with beavers was discovered to the west, across the Atlantic Ocean. The discovery of an entirely new world inhabited by unknown beasts, birds and plants jolted the European imagination and kick-started a vibrant interest in the natural world. Naturalists began to look at all animals – even well-known creatures – with fresh eyes. No doubt they would have examined Eurasian beavers if they were not so exceedingly hard to find. But as it was, the North American beaver received all the attention.

The natural habitat of North American beavers stretches from the Pacific Ocean to the Atlantic and from Canada to northern Mexico, with the exception of the treeless arctic tundra, the deserts of the southwestern United States and the alligator-infested bayous of Florida. No one knows quite how many beavers once occupied North America, but we can make a guess. The combined area of Canada and the United States is almost 20 million km² (7.7 million sq. miles). Subtracting a generous 5 million km² (1.9 million sq. miles) for the uninhabitable arctic, deserts, mountain peaks and alligator-infested rivers, leaves 15 million km² (5.8 million sq.

miles). If one lodge of six beavers occupied each square kilometre, the numbers would be astonishing.

Yet despite the animal's superabundance, early natural histories continued the trope of the hard-to-see beaver. After four years in the Massachusetts Bay Colony between 1629 and 1633, William Wood described beavers as having 'feet like a Mole before, and behinde like a Goose . . . his head is something like an Otters head, saving that his teeth before be placed like the teeth of a Rabbet'.[13] Another New World description compares the beaver's various parts to those of otters, basset hounds, rats, cats, rabbits, pigs, carp, geese and squirrels.[14] The seventeenth-century Acadian Nicolas Denys claimed beavers were a species of fish that resembled shorn sheep. Even Mortimer offers the typical animal inventory to describe Sloane's beaver. Except for her tail, she very much resembled a 'great over-grown Water-Rat'. She ate like a squirrel. Her hind feet were webbed like those of a goose. On dry land she waddled 'like a Duck' but she swam 'much swifter than any Water-Fowl, moving underwater as swift, I believe, as a Carp'.[15] Part fish, part waterfowl, part rodent, the beaver blurred between animal kingdoms – at least on the outside.

As for beaver insides, detailed anatomical descriptions of any animal were rare until the end of the seventeenth century, and most early natural histories paid little attention to the internal structure of animals. Mortimer's account of Sloane's beaver is among the first detailed inspections of the anatomical particularity of a female beaver. She had been torn apart by a dog, and her body was surely a bloodied clutter of tubes and organs, but evidently Mortimer looked long and hard at what remained. He describes her bowels and ovaries as resembling those of a bitch, while her bladder was the size of a wrinkled walnut. Her two castor sacs were like two small pears, filled with a dark, syrupy, potently musky tar. The anal scent glands were oblong, knobby

With human-like hands, a hump-back and fishy tail, the beaver was explained as a hodgepodge of creaturely parts.

and the pale fleshy colour of a pancreas. Each anal gland was connected to a castor sac above and to the dark orifice below, beset with long black hairs. The accompanying illustration is equally precise, neatly delineating all her parts. Mortimer even included a portion of her tail so readers could orientate themselves, anatomically speaking, which is helpful as the genitalia float in space and share the page with a technical diagram of a new instrument capable of taking a ship's latitude during cloudy weather, when the horizon was not visible. In other words, although Mortimer's observations were obviously drawn from the life and death of a real beaver, the only image he was able to offer his readers was, once again, a disjointed animal from a distant, foggy geography.

Natural history illustrations had their own befogged lineage, and Mortimer's illustration can be traced to another beaver back-end observed in Paris about half a century earlier by Claude Perrault.

One of the founding members of the Royal Academy of Sciences in Paris, Perrault organized regular dissections of the animals that died in Louis XIV's royal menagerie at Versailles and in 1669 published a small volume of his anatomical investigations of five dead beasts: a chameleon, a dromedary, a bear, a gazelle and a male beaver.

The beaver had been captured in the Saint Lawrence River and had lived for several years in the menagerie before succumbing to an unknown illness. Perrault begins his autopsy report by acknowledging how little known beaver biology remained:

> It is so much the more necessary to observe exactly all the Parts of the beaver because an exact description has never been made. The Ancients said almost nothing of this animal, and the moderns have been more drawn to talking about its nature than examining the structure of its body.[16]

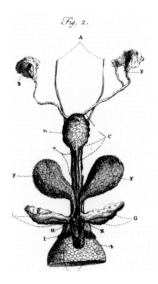

Fig. 2.

Cromwell Mortimer's drawing of the inner parts of a female beaver. BB indicates 'The *Ovaria*', FF 'the two *Glandules*, containing the *Castor*' and I 'the *Vagina* cut off.'

True to his word, Perrault described each and every part of the beaver from its tail to its optic nerves, although he was unable to observe the colour of its eyes as they were eaten by Versailles rats before the animal's death was discovered. The accompanying illustrations demonstrated various important beaver bits – front paw, brain, sharp-pointed penis bone, colon and caecum, and pelvis – which hover on the page above a solitary beaver, crouching uneasily in an Italianate country scene. And with his awkward, waterless creature, even Perrault's beaver withdraws from lived reality: the illustration was just another copy of a long-dead beaver.

Perrault based his beaver illustration on that found in Conrad Gessner's *Historiae animalium*, published in four volumes between 1551 and 1558. The work was a massive scholarly achievement, and both the text and images remained the zoological references for the next 200 years. Unlike the dogs of medieval bestiaries or the heraldic wolf-beavers, Gessner's beaver has all the proper beaver features. Note its shaggy fur, large incisors, small ears and eyes, waffle tail, webbed hind feet and clawed forepaws. But the animal's elongated body gives the beaver away: they are telltale signs of the crude practices of early taxidermy. Nevertheless, for the next two centuries every beaver illustrated in a natural history, dictionary or travel narrative was based on Gessner's image – which is to say, the most authoritative beaver circulating among Enlightenment naturalists was drawn from a roughly stuffed, overstretched beaver pelt. It was not until 1760, in the sixth volume of Buffon's 6,000-page encyclopaedia of natural history, that an accurately humpbacked, podgy beaver was finally depicted.

For an animal that has been consistently misrepresented, disassembled and explained as an amalgamation of creaturely life, the living beaver is actually a marvel of biological unity. Each and every facet of a beaver's biology and social behaviour is adapted to the requirements of transforming landscapes and

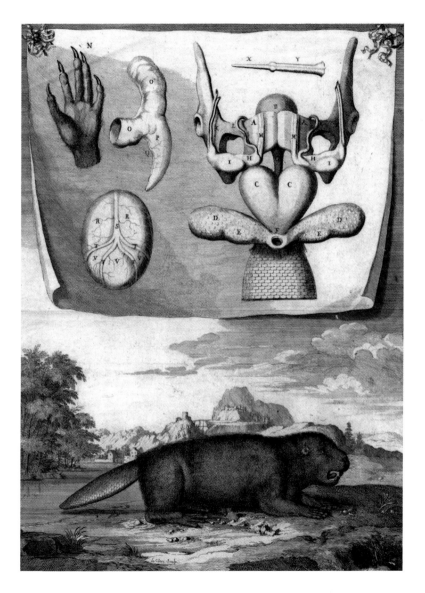

The beaver is illustrated with mouth open to reveal its large teeth with its tail flipped vertically to display the textural pattern. From Conrad Gessner, *Historiae animalium* (1551–87).

DE CASTORE.

A.

CASTOR animal quadrupes est amphibiū: Latini fibrum, & ut Seruio placet canē Ponticum uocant, Græcis nominatur castor, & κύωρ πόντιος, id est, canis fluuiatilis, ut apud Syluaticum legimus. Italis, biuaro: uel beuero: Gallis, bieure, quanquā Brasauola Gallos Castoris nomē retinere scribit:id quod Hispanos fecisse puto:fieri tamen potest ut Galli etiam in regionibus quibusdam re tinuerint. In Matthæoli Italica Dioscoridis trāslatione fiber ipse il castoreo uocatur.Germanis biber:Anglis beuer.Illyrijs bobr: quæ omnia à fibro uoce Latina deducta esse prima fronte statim apparet.Syluaticus plurima passim castoris & castorei in Arabum libris nomina recenset, quorum multa scriptura solum & orthographia differūt, ego omnia ut cunq corrupta adnumerabo,Albeduester,castoreum: ego ipsum castorem potius intelligo, nam pro testiculis tum uel iune uel similem uocem addere solent; Ium debedust, Iune da baduster:Angul de beldustor:Guidelarus : Quibar:In de bidister;Zun de beduster:Iune da bauster:Iune de bustor ; Gen de beduster. Auicēna habet Giědedestar,aliâs Giendibidestar. Reperio & alia quædam uocabula apud Syluaticum & alios, quæ tum inter se tum à superioribus non parum differunt;ut, Cascubas,Amphima, uoce corrupta forsan ab amphibio: & Anfinia similiter, nam ceu Græcam Syluaticus exponit;item Achiam,Anchian, Anchiani,Antin algil,Asuschelhar.Albertus Iamyekyz barbaram uocem, ex Auicēna putto, castorem interpretatur: quæ uox sortassis Illyrica est. Nam Polonis dama Ianij dicitur, cuius diminutiuum Ianijska. Castoreum testiculus est animalis , quod castor appellal uel deū, Platearius. Ex his tot scribendi modis quin maior pars corrupta sit, dubiū non est:ego quos quibus præferam incertus sum. Kipod Hebraicâ uocem Esaiæ 34. & alibi in Sacris literis non castorem, ut cuidam uidetur,sed echinum terrestrem significare in eius historia demonstrabo. אנקה anakah Leuitici cap. 11. aliqui ericium,alij hirudinem interpretantur, au thor concordantiarum reptile uolans.R.Salomon alibi hericium , alibi אבבב exponit, id est fibrum, Gallica lingua (qua is uti solet) bieure dictum : sic etiam Munsterus legit. Non placet legi uiuerṛ, quod id uocabulum lingua Gallica R.Salomoni familiari,aliter efferatur.

B.

Differt à lutra fiber cauda solum:cætero pilus utriq pluma mollior:utriq aquaticum, Plinius. Sunt qui fibrum meli comparent:sed corpus ei longius tribuunt, & pilum subtiliorem. Pilos habet pulchros,

LE BIEVRE.

building dams, canals and lodges. From anatomical goggles and fur-lined lips to lifelong monogamy and exceptionally pungent musk, the beaver is extraordinarily equipped to thrive within its self-made wetland ecosystem. 'If I could design the perfect animal,' Glynnis Hood writes in her beaver manifesto, 'it would be the beaver.'[17]

Another version of Conrad Gessner's beaver, from Guillaume Rondelet's *L'Histoire entière des poissons* (1558).

THE ANATOMICAL BEAVER

Beavers have been known for their musk, their fur and their architectural prowess, but to scientists, beavers are classified by their teeth. Along with rats, agoutis, hamsters, mice, squirrels, jerboas, capybaras and porcupines, beavers belong to the mammalian order Rodentia, or 'gnawers', from the Latin *rodere*, to gnaw. True to their name, all rodents except one are distinguished by a single pair of continuously growing upper and lower incisors, which the animals keep short and sharp by breaking open nuts, chewing wood and bark, or gnawing into attics and basements. And all

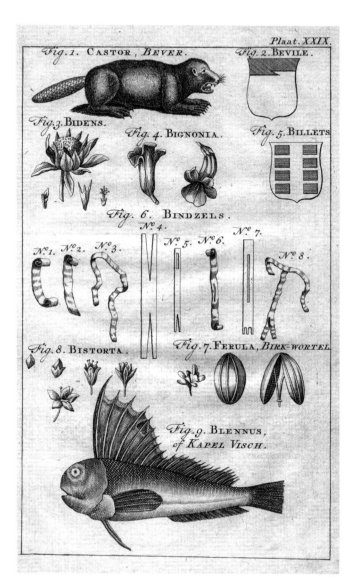

Fig.1. CASTOR, BEVER.

Fig.2. BEVILE.

Fig.3. BIDENS.

Fig.4. BIGNONIA.

Fig.5. BILLETS

Fig.6. BINDZELS.

N.º 4.

N.º 1. N.º 2. N.º 3. N.º 5. N.º 6. N.º 7.

N.º 8.

Fig.8. BISTORTA.

Fig.7. FERULA, BIRK-WORTEL

Fig.9. BLENNUS, of KAPEL VISCH.

Buffon's beaver launched a new epoch of naturalistic beaver illustrations.

rodents except one lack canine teeth (a gummy gap remains where the canines would be), followed by one or more molars endowed with whirled ridges of enamel to increase their grinding power. The exception is an Indonesian shrew-rat, unknown to science until 2011. *Paucidentomys vermidax*, translatable as 'worm-eating few-toothed mouse', lacks the ability to chew at all since its only teeth are two upper incisors. It lives on a strict diet of earthworms.

Things beginning with the letter 'B', from an 18th-century Dutch encyclopaedia.

1. Blindmaus.(Spalax.)
2. Taschenratte.(Saccomys.)
3. Blaumoll.(Bathyergus.)
4. Hamster.
5. Stachelratte.(Loncheres.)
6. Bisamratte.(Ondatra.)
7. Sumpfratte.(Hydromys.)
8. Sumpfbiber.(Myopotamus.)
9. Biber.(Castor.)
5. Stachelschwein.(Hystrix.)

1. Kletterratte.(Jaculus.)
4. Hamster.
3. Schlafratte.(Glis.)
1. Fischeichhorn.(Sciurus.)
7. Aguti.

1. Springmaus.(Dipus.)
2. Murmelthier.(Arctomys.)
2. Springhase.(Pedetes.)
3. Wollhase.(Chinchilla.)
4. Viscacha.
6. Cavyhare.
Hase.(Lepus.)

The vast majority of rodent incisors have evolved into highly efficient, self-sharpening instruments, capable of chewing through the hardest materials. The teeth are composed of two layers, a hard enamel at the front and a softer dentine at the back. When the animals gnaw, the upper and lower incisors slice against each other like a pair of scissors. As the softer dentine wears away, the enamel is filed into razor-sharp chisels. The more a rodent gnaws, the sharper its teeth become. But ever-growing teeth have their drawbacks; if a beaver happens to lose an incisor, or if the upper and lower teeth fail to meet and grind against one another, dental havoc results. Without an upper tooth to keep it in check, a lower incisor can grow in an upward curve until it pierces the skull.

The rodent family as illustrated in Lorenz Oken's *Natural History for All Classes* (1833–41).

Rodent-like animals appeared in the Palaeocene, just a few million years after the great extinction event that ended the age of the dinosaurs 65 million years ago. Around 54 million years ago, the earliest beaver-like animals diverged from their closest ancestor. This impressively long evolutionary history may explain some of the beaver's peculiarities.

Extensive fossil records indicate that castorids (as the beaver family is known) were once a large and diverse family. At least 30 different genera have been isolated and four beaver subfamilies are generally agreed on. Early castorids vary in size, from small-bodied burrowers to Ice Age giants that weighed as much as black bears and lived in swamps. They ranged throughout both the North American and Eurasian continents, from the high Arctic to a southerly boundary of Florida and Thailand.

From the shape of various bones and teeth, and from dental wear, scientists believe castorids can be divided into two main evolutionary branches, or clades: a burrowing clade and a semi-aquatic clade. Burrowing castorids have short necks, small tails, robust forelimbs and large claws adapted for digging. Aquatic adaptations include shortened femurs, enlarged hind feet, a foot

An overgrown lower incisor which continued to grow in a complete circle, re-entering the animal's mouth through its cheek.

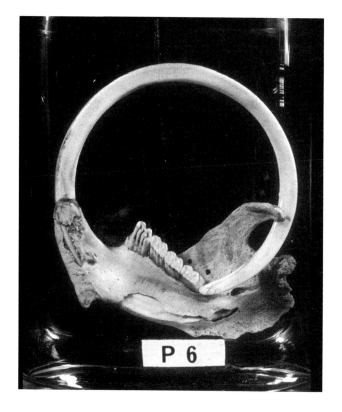

P 6

shape consistent with the presence of webbing, flattened vertebrae in the tail (specialized for swimming) and a grooming claw on the hind feet, which modern beavers use to maintain their water-proof fur. Fossil evidence also suggests that burrowing beavers inhabited arid environments while, naturally enough, swimming castorids lived in wetter landscapes. Since all castorids burrow (even modern beavers burrow into river banks and excavate long canals for transporting building materials), burrowing is likely to be castorids' most primitive behaviour. Swimming is believed to have evolved only once in the semiaquatic clade. It goes without saying that one lineage was more successful than the other.

The earliest castorid belonged to the subfamily Agnotocasto-rinae. Fossils dating to the late Eocene and early Oligocene (40–36 MYA) have been found throughout North America and several sites in Europe and Asia. The suffix *agnoto* means unknown, which is appropriate. Beyond its geographic range, little is known about the subfamily's behaviour, particularly whether the animals could

The third toe on a beaver's hind foot has a split toenail comb, which the animal uses to keep its fur clean and waterproof.

swim or not: although remains are often found in pond deposits, the fossils do not suggest it was a swimmer. The other three beaver subfamilies offer a clearer biological story.

Palaeocastorinae were burrowers and included the distinguished burrower *Palaocastor*. *Palaocastor* lived throughout the North American Badlands in the late Oligocene (25 MYA). They were small, about the size of a muskrat, with massive forelimbs, enlarged forepaws and protruding chisel-like teeth with which they dug giant corkscrew burrows, known throughout the Dakotas and Nebraska as 'devil's corkscrews'. Often as deep as 3 m (10 ft), the corkscrews were long believed to be fossils of freshwater sponges as it seemed impossible that an animal would or could create such bizarre formations. It was not until a fossilized beaver was found in a burrow that the true creator was known.

The other two subfamilies, Castoroidinae and Castorinae, were swimmers. At least 24 million years ago, their common ancestor evolved swimming skills and also the ability to harvest wood.[18] The secret to the beaver's evolutionary success lies in the combined power of those two skills.

Unlike burrowing castorids, which were confined to North America, the swimming clade lived throughout Eurasia and North America and seems to have spread back and forth via the Beringian isthmus, an Arctic land bridge between modern-day Russia and Alaska. Castoroidinae included two giant beavers, *Castoroides* and *Trogontherium*. Both appear to have originated in North America at least 23 million years ago with *Trogontherium* migrating almost immediately to Eurasia. *Castoroides* was the largest rodent ever known to exist in North America. They grew over 2.5 m (8 ft) in length, weighed up to 100 kg (220 lb) and died out 10,000 years ago, at the end of the last ice age, along with woolly mammoths and mastodons. Ten thousand years is not so long ago, and North American legends are filled with fascinating stories of giant beavers. Ojibwa tell how the broken dam of the giant beaver Waub-Ameek formed the waterway and chain of islands between Lake Huron and Lake Superior. The Dene people of Great Slave Lake and Artillery Lake tell of a hunter named Xachogh who killed giant beavers to feed his people. And the Pocumtuck tribe in the Connecticut River valley have a legend of a giant beaver that came ashore to devour people when the river ran dry of fish. The tribe called on the benevolent spirit Hobomock, who chased the giant beaver into the water and killed it with a large stick. The hills of Pocumtuck range are his petrified remains.

Both living beaver species (genus *Castor*) belong to the subfamily Castorinae. Castorinae also includes the oldest-known woodcutting and swimming castorid, *Steneofiber eseri*, which appeared in the earliest Miocene, about 23 million years ago.

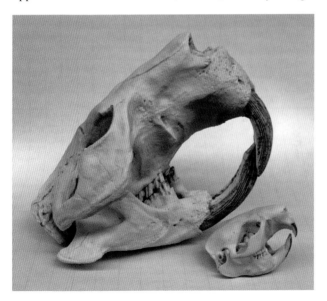

A giant beaver skull measures approximately 12 in. (30 cm) in length. The skull of a modern beaver is closer to 4 in. (10 cm).

That castorids seem to have co-evolved swimming and wood-cutting skills during the Miocene is significant. Sandwiched between the warmer Oligocene and the cooler Pliocene, the Miocene is characterized by a series of cooling trends. By the middle of the Miocene, the Arctic region endured harsh winters, with high snow accumulation and frozen lakes. But semiaquatic castorids do not seem to have been adversely affected by the hard winters. In fact, they may have thrived. In contrast to their burrowing relatives, semiaquatic castorids derived food and shelter from trees and protection within the water. Although we cannot be sure how prehistoric castorids survived, the winter habits of modern beavers perhaps give us a clue.

A beaver's lodge can be 12 m (40 ft) across, 3 m (10 ft) high and have more than 3,000 kg (6,000 lb) of logs and mud. Such an enormous structure has several distinct advantages: first, the

During hard northern winters, beavers can survive under the ice for months thanks to their cache of branches.

interior cavity of lodges, insulated by surrounding water and snow, are warmer than burrows. Lodges are also more protected. Wolves, bobcats, mountain lions and other predators cannot dig beavers out, and because beavers build their entrances underwater, they can come and go unseen. (Beavers are slow and lumbering on land; their main defence is to slip quickly and quietly into deep water where predators cannot follow.) Beavers also use logs, branches and mud to dam rivers, which allows them to control the water level and ensure it does not drop too low, compromising safety, or rise too high, flooding the interior of their lodge.

Beavers have also solved the dilemma of winter sustenance. When deep snow covers vegetation, herbivores must either hibernate or find a way to get food during the long winter months. Perhaps because they live so close to the water and must remain ever-vigilant against flooding, beavers do not hibernate. Rather ingeniously, at the first sign of frost they begin stocking an underwater larder by planting large branches in the mud near the entrance of their lodge. When winter comes and the pond freezes, beavers will be locked under the ice. But because their entrances are underwater, beavers can swim out in complete safety to choose a favourite twig. Usually a few branches of the larder poke out from the water and accumulate an insulating layer of snow. The snow keeps the water from freezing in and around the food pile and also provides a breathing hole when beavers are outside their lodge. (Beavers will also make a break in their dam, if necessary, to drain some water and provide breathing space under the ice.) If lodge construction and underwater winter food caching, both of which presuppose swimming and woodcutting abilities, did coevolve during the long, cold Miocene winters, it seems quite likely that castorids developed a good thing a very long time ago and have been perfecting their skills ever since.

The oldest *Castor* fossils are those of *Castor neglectus* from Germany, 10–12 million years old. Fossils of a shared ancestor who lived 8 million years ago have been found on both continents, and the speciation of *Castor fiber* (the Eurasian beaver) and *Castor canadensis* (the North American beaver) likely occurred over 7 million years ago.

The two species are genetically incompatible – the North American species has 40 chromosomes while Eurasian beavers have 48 – and are unable to produce viable offspring. Yet despite the millions of years of separation, the two beavers are all but identical in shape, size and behaviour. Eurasian beavers have smaller skulls and narrower tails while the North American species is more aggressive and can be slightly larger. Their differences are so minor that it was only genetic testing that conclusively determined there were two beavers, not one. In other words, modern beavers have remained virtually unchanged since before the two species diverged, at least 8 million years ago. In fact, living beavers are nearly indistinguishable from their ancient relatives, including *Castor neglectus*, which lived 12 million years ago. The time scale is extraordinary. And while beavers are not as old as those supreme evolutionary survivors such as sharks, crocodiles and cockroaches, just give them time.

Beavers could have evolved any number of different traits and behaviours. They could have adapted to live in fallen trees, to build lodges on dry land, or to have acquired better defensive skills. There is no necessary reason for beavers to have evolved as they did, and I do not mean to suggest a just-so story of beaver evolution. But while beavers are just another example of millions of years of biological chance and accident, they are something of an evolutionary wonder. All creaturely life has evolved traits and features by which it manages to survive. But the beaver has evolved to do more than survive; or rather, survival in beaver terms

involves elaborate architectural creations and sophisticated water management. The beaver is built to build.

A beaver's entire existence revolves around those two fundamental adaptions: woodcutting and swimming. A very large skull and powerful jaw muscles provide the chainsaw power to the beaver's chisel teeth, but without the ability to swim and transport logs by water, felled trees would be all but useless. Certainly beavers are not diminutive. The world's second largest rodent (after the South American capybara), adult beavers measure over a meter in length and weigh about 20 kg (44 lb). Even bigger beavers have been documented. A beaver in Missouri was recorded at 43.6 kg (96 lb) and another in Wisconsin topped the scales at 50 kg (110 lb).[19] But still, dragging dozens of logs through the forest is arduous work even for a robust animal, and noisy enough to attract unwelcome attention. Instead beavers transport logs by water, and when there is no water nearby, they dig a network of canals. In other words, by learning to exploit water transportation, beavers unleashed the power of their teeth.

A near-invisible beaver transports a leafy branch.

Measuring a beaver's tail.

Beavers come alive in water, and their most fascinating adaptations are built for an aquatic life. A beaver's eyes, ears and nose are aligned in a row, high on their heads, so they can swim almost completely submerged while logs seem to move along as if by an invisible hand. Beavers have fur-lined lips – unique among animals. The lips close behind the incisors, allowing beavers to swim while holding branches in their teeth without swallowing water. Part of the tongue and epiglottis also prevent beavers from swallowing water. They have valvular noses and ears which close tightly when they are underwater, and nictitating membranes – a third eyelid that acts as swimming goggles. The membrane changes the curvature of the eyes, adjusting the vision to underwater refraction. Their hind feet are completely webbed to the roots of the claws and can spread wider than a large man's hand, making beavers powerful swimmers and divers.

As medieval theologians suspected, a beaver's tail is an extraordinary appendage, a sort of anatomical Swiss Army knife with a use for every aspect of the animal's lifestyle. In the water, the tail is a rudder and flipper. On dry land, it acts as a ballast, stabilizing the beaver as it chews down trees or waddles on its hind feet with an armload of mud. It is a warning signal; at the first sign or smell of danger, beavers slap their tail on water, warning other beavers of intruders. The tail is also a fat reserve for the long winter months, and through a counter-current arrangement of blood vessels, acts as a thermoregulator. About 25 per cent of body heat is lost through the tail in summer, allowing the exceptionally hairy beaver to stay cool. In winter, as beavers swim through icy waters, less blood flows through the tail, reducing the heat loss to 2 per cent.

A family of beavers enjoying a meal.

Each and every facet of a beaver's biology and social behaviour is adapted to maintaining its watery estate. Beavers' front paws, for example, are useless for swimming, but perfect for building. The nimble, hand-like paws dextrously weave branches together and pat the mud solid on their dams and lodges. Beavers also mate for life – a rarity among animals – otherwise each spring a pair would split, and one would drive the other away, forcing it to begin the entire building process again. And, in contrast with most rodents, beavers have relatively small litters of two to four kits and do not become sexually mature until their second year. (Consider that the Nuttall's cottontail rabbit has up to five litters each breeding season; Norway rats are sexually mature at eleven weeks; and deer mice are able to breed within thirty days.) Lifelong pair bonding and a low reproductive rate makes good sense for the architecturally inclined, and a late sexual maturity means that two-year-old kits help care for the yearlings while their parents maintain the dam and lodge and store up food for the coming winter.

Beavers also have a tremendous sense of ownership. Many animals have sebaceous anal scent glands which they use for territorial marking. But only beavers have a second pair of scent organs – their castoreum-producing castor sacs. Beavers are also the only mammals known to build a structure for their territorial scent markings, a sort of large mud pie formed from mud dredged up from the pond. Holding the mud to its chest with its forepaws, a beaver will waddle a few steps from the water's edge and deposit the mud in a mound. It then straddles the mound and excretes castoreum or anal gland secretions or both. (Apparently this excreting is audible from close by.) The mound might be a single load or can be rather sizeable. The largest scent mound on record is 80 cm (2 ft 7 in.) wide and 50 cm (1 ft 8 in.) high and was found at Cranberry Lake in New York's Adirondack Mountains. Building a mound raises the beaver's scent, a clever tactic in areas prone to flooding, and helps waft it further afield. The wet mud likely also intensifies the smell of castoreum, rather like the strong 'dog' smell of a wet dog.

Because beavers mate for life and do not use their musk for sexual advertisement, their scent could not carry a clearer message: *this place is occupied*. But if a beaver's scent is meant to repel and ward off interloping beavers, it has exuded a strangely magnetic attraction for humans. For millennia, the beaver's scent has been used as perfume, medicine, food flavouring and, above all, for storytelling.

Mortimer gave his paper a seemingly straightforward title, 'The Anatomy of a Female Beaver, and an Account of Castor Found in Her'. A century earlier the title would have been remarkable. Castor sacs were long believed to be a beaver's testicles. In other words, if castor (better known today as castoreum) were found in a female beaver, it would have revealed her to be a hermaphrodite. In fact, Mortimer began his paper by deriding an anatomist identified as E.G.H. who committed precisely such an error while dissecting a male and female in 1684. (Oddly, E.G.H. mistook the male for the hermaphrodite.)

Mortimer was at the tail end of the ancient anatomical confusion, but he could not help repeating the bawdy tale of self-castration inspired by the beaver's scent organs. Perhaps the story would have been less intoxicating if the beaver's scent were not so potent, but what began as a musky territorial warning was transformed into a tenacious set of beliefs inspired by an ancient fable known as 'The Beaver and his Testicles'. And so we begin our first beaver romance: musk.

2 Musk

These Beasts bite off their Pizzles and throw them to
the Hunter, which are an exceedingly good Medicine
to help Abortion, stop the monthly flowers, [and] Giddiness
in the Head.

John Ogilby, *America: Being an Accurate Description of the New World*
(1670)

In 1768, an Edinburgh surgeon named William Alexander
began a series of self-administered pharmaceutical trials to test
the efficacy of various time-honoured medicines. Among the
tonics, sudorifics, antiseptics and diuretics was castoreum, the
musky secretions from beavers' scent organs. Since ancient times
castoreum had been used as a potent stimulant and antispasmodic, prescribed mainly to women suffering from infertility,
amenorrhea, unwanted pregnancies and, most particularly,
hysteria.

Alexander began with a small dose – ten grains – and gradually
increased his daily dosage until he reached two drams (about 8 g).
Over the week, he observed no other physiological effect than 'a
few disagreeable eructations' and concluded that castoreum was
useless and 'ill deserving of a place in the present catalogue of
medicines'.[1] (He came to the same conclusion about saffron which
he tested after learning a lunatic had swallowed a very large quantity without any adverse effects.) In 1822, Dr J.C.G. Jörg of Leipzig
repeated Alexander's trials, this time including three women
among his 26 test subjects. They all came to the same conclusion:
castoreum's only effects were unpleasant belches which persisted
through the day and smelled of musky beaver.[2]

Some physicians contested the evidence, even into the nineteenth century. John Eberle, an American physician practising

in Pennsylvania, argued that healthy bodies were poor test subjects as they did not respond to medication as bodies in a weakened state. Castoreum, Eberle argued, remained an excellent tonic for hysterical women, especially those with 'delicate and irritable habits'. Far from being inert, beaver musk was sufficiently potent to cause 'very unpleasant symptoms' such as oppressed breathing, flushed face, dry skin and anxiety in the region of the heart. However, Eberle did concede that the medicine was only successful in very large doses – two to three spoonfuls – and was even more effective when administered with laudanum.[3]

The theory that castoreum was good for uterine complaints and hysterical women is made more curious by the medicine's supposed source: beaver musk was long believed to originate in a beaver's testicles.

Of all the myths and marvels surrounding the beaver, the oldest and surely the strangest centres on his testicles and his curious act of self-preservation. The tale dates from at least the sixth century BC, and is likely much older still, but the earliest version comes to us from Aesop, who put it like this:

> It is said that when the beaver is being chased by dogs and realizes that he cannot outrun them, he bites off his testicles, since he knows that this is what he is hunted for. I suppose there is some kind of superhuman understanding that prompts the beaver to act in this way, for as soon as the hunter lays his hands on that magical medicine, he abandons the chase and calls off his dogs.

All three parts of the fable were common knowledge and held as truth well into the sixteenth century. First, castoreum was believed to have significant healing properties. The potent-smelling, yellowish, sticky secretion was thought to be produced in the animal's

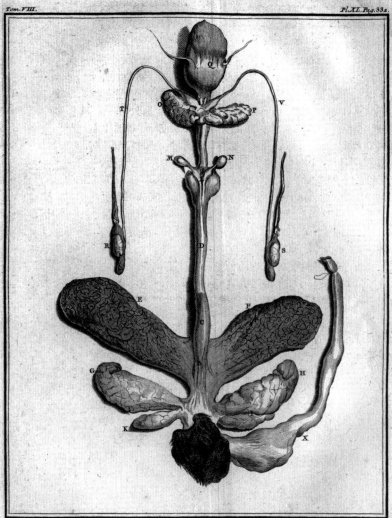

testicles. And, most astonishing of all, the beaver, knowing the value of his testicles, bit them off to save his life. Even more bizarre is the pithy moral Aesop was able to wring from a self-castrating beaver. As he put it: 'If only people would take the same approach and agree to be deprived of their possessions in order to live lives free from danger; no one, after all, would set a trap for someone already stripped to the skin.'[4] Two thousand years later, on the other side of the world, Aesop's moral would prove darkly ironic. Rather than beavers sacrificing their musk to save their skins, beaver musk was used as an intoxicating lure to trap beavers for their skins.

The scent organs and reproductive system of a male beaver.

To state the obvious, castoreum is not a species of beaver semen, nor do beavers geld themselves. The fable is only tenuously attached to the beaver by the power of its scent, yet its musky untruths proved intoxicating to any culture they wafted through.

Chased by a hunter's dog, the beaver divests himself of his testicles with one swift bite.

Just as Aesop may have drawn on an ancient Egyptian legend, his tale passed into Roman folklore and ethical discourses. It was absorbed into scientific literature by the encyclopaedists Pliny the Elder and Claudius Aelianus, whose texts were among the most widely quoted natural histories throughout the Renaissance. The fable passed into the early Christian canon of spiritual teaching. It was translated into virtually every European vernacular. The seventh-century scholar Isidore of Seville added an etymological elegancy to the tale by erroneously claiming that the word *castor* was derived from the Latin verb *castrare*, to castrate. (In fact, the Latin word for beaver is *fiber*; *castor* is the Greek. For better or worse, when the great eighteenth-century systemizer Carl Linnaeus gave the Eurasian beaver the binomial name *Castor fiber*, he essentially named it beaver beaver.)

Sometime before his death in 1566 from a surfeit of figs, the French physician Guillaume Rondelet dissected a beaver with sufficient accuracy to determine that castoreum was produced by scent organs held inside the beaver's abdomen, and not by outward hanging testicles. (In fact, since the beaver's genuine testicles are also held inside the body, a living beaver can only be sexed by feeling for its hidden penis bone.) And in 1668 the French apothecary Moyse Charas dismissed the entire idea of the fable as an anatomical impossibility: beavers were far too fat in the middle. With a touch of barnyard whimsy, Charas declared that self-castration 'would be as impossible for him to accomplish as for a pig'.[5]

As might be expected when hunting a scent, tracking the fables and fabrications surrounding castoreum leads into outlandish territories. Ancient animal tales, Christian moralism, gynaeco-logical myths, and fur trapping in the North American wilderness layer up like an intoxicating perfume that ultimately climaxes with the obliteration of the beaver.

Testicles and aromatic musk were deeply entwined in the ancient world. The word 'musk' comes from the ancient Persian word for testicle, *muska*, which is derived from the Indo-European root for mouse, *mus*. The etymological link between musk, testicles and mice can likely be traced to the musk pods of the male musk deer, the most celebrated source of animal notes in perfumery: the pods are round and furry like a mouse and hang between the deer's navel and penis. Beavers are also entangled in the musky etymology. The Sanskrit word for musk is *kasturi*, derived from the Greek words for beaver, *castor*, and its potent-smelling secretion, *castoreum*.[6]

The ancients can hardly be blamed for confusing the beaver's scent organs with its testes. Its anal scent glands are located just under the skin in the region one would expect to find testicles, between the base of the tail and the cloaca, or a beaver's single rear vent. The glands can bulge externally when in use and are connected to the beaver's urogenital tract. Once removed they resemble nothing so much as a pair of dried, dark liverish-brown testicles.

All carnivores, including humans, have anal scent glands. Many species of snakes also have musk-secreting glands around their cloaca, as do crocodiles which have a second pair in their lower jaw. Such sebaceous glands produce an unctuous and musky substance called sebum, which animals use to attract mates and mark territory. Waterfowl and aquatic mammals also use the oily secretions to waterproof their fur.

Dried castor sacs resemble nothing so much as a pair of dried testicles united by a spermatic cord.

58

However, beavers are uniquely endowed with a second pair of scent organs – the castor sacs – which are not glands but large pouches filled with densely packed layers of fibrous epithelium. Castor sacs are larger than the beaver's anal glands and weigh 0.3 per cent of the beaver's body weight, or about 60 g (2 oz). Both sexes possess both anal glands and castor sacs, and the two fluids are used for territorial marking. Like the anal scent glands, the castor sacs are connected to the urogenital tract and resemble two large, wizened testicles. But unlike the anal glands, castor sacs do not have a sphincter, which means castoreum is not excreted so much as leaked out whenever the beaver urinates.

Technically speaking, castoreum is precisely that – the contents of the castor sacs mixed with urine. But over the centuries, any part or fluid of either the anal glands or castor sacs has been marketed as castoreum, and likely a few bits of anatomy besides. Because it was usually an import, castoreum was an expensive medicine, and its long history has been plagued by adulteration. In the first century AD, Pliny the Elder described the common practice of substituting beaver kidneys, containing a mixture of 'gum and blood', for the 'genuine testes'.[7] More than 1,500 years later, Richard Hakluyt, that great Elizabethan relater of adventurous tales, described a test by which Persian traders confirmed the quality of their castoreum: if a deep inhalation made your nose bleed, the castoreum was pure. As late as 1825, *The American Dispensatory* cautioned against a counterfeit composed of gummy resins stuffed into the scrotum of a goat, which bring us back to the dark little fable of the self-castrating beaver.

Perhaps ancient beaver hunters truly believed that castor sacs were the animals' testicles. But did they ever wonder why every beaver they caught was a male? Or why beavers had multiple testicles, if the anal scent glands and genuine testes were also counted? Admittedly, such anatomical particularities were hardly

A shorn female beaver with teats, showing that both sexes have castor sacs.

unusual in the ancient and Renaissance world view. Plenty of oddly romantic stories circulated about other animals, both exotic and local. For example, it was commonly held that all hares were hermaphrodites, that the flesh of peacocks was incorruptible, that badgers had legs shorter on one side of their body than the other and, of course, that a cornered beaver was wily enough to save his life by any means possible.

It is worth noting that the Roman physician-philosopher Sextius Niger discredited the fable in the first century AD. Moreover, Pliny gave full credence to Sextius' anatomical investigations. In his entry on castoreum in *Naturalis historia*, Pliny wrote that Sextius, 'a most careful enquirer into the nature and history of medicinal substances', disproved the fable as anatomically untrue.[8] And yet the tale lingered; it was too deliciously perverse to cast aside simply on the opinion of one careful observer.

Among Leonardo da Vinci's notebooks is a series of short allegories and ancient wisdoms of the animal kingdom. 'The bite of the tarantula fixes a man's mind on one idea', Leonardo writes, 'that is on the thing he was thinking when he was bitten.' Of the swan, 'it sings sweetly as it dies, its life ending with that song', while the grasshopper 'dies in oil and revives in vinegar'. The majority are moral fables, each titled by the virtue or vice the animal's character exemplifies. Cheerfulness is proper to the cock, who rejoices over every little thing. Folly is the bull who, having a horror of red, rushes at a tree that hunters have dressed in red fabric, and thus with horns rammed into the trunk is easily killed. And Peace is the beaver: 'We read of the beaver that when it is pursued, knowing that it is for the virtue in its medicinal testicles and not being able to escape, it stops; and to be at peace with its pursuers, it bites off its testicles with its sharp teeth, and leaves them to its enemies.'[9]

Leonardo's emphasis on the sharpness of a beaver's teeth is unique. Perhaps his keen understanding of anatomy made him ponder just how such a feat could be accomplished. And although no author ever wrote this, perhaps the fable was inspired as much by the beaver's remarkable incisors as by its musk. The beaver's oversized, razor-sharp teeth could be interpreted as a divinely created endowment, perfectly suited to the act of self-castration.

From sharp-toothed ferocity to the ensuring tranquillity, the beaver offered two very different emotional states, and bestiaries and books of fables pictured beavers in a variety of canine forms. The fiercest wolfish beavers are depicted in the act of biting themselves. A steely grimace would certainly befit the act, which was performed, as one version of the fable put it, 'with a great resolution and presence of mind'.[10] After the act, however, the beaver was forever free from persecution. In a fifteenth-century Florentine manuscript of Aesop's fables owned by the Medicis, a dachshund-like beaver scurries away from hunters to live out his life in tranquillity.

The beaver's desire 'to be at peace', as Leonardo put it, was only one of many virtues gleaned from the tale. A gentle creature, endowed with the determination to divest himself of his most treasured possession, the beaver was variously interpreted as the animal epitome of pragmatism, thriftiness, austerity, self-denial and chastity.

The Cynics viewed the beaver as the perfect ascetic: his act of self-preservation exemplified their emphasis on life and freedom at all costs. The satirist Juvenal used the beaver as a symbol of prudence. In Satire 12, Juvenal writes of a terrible storm at sea threatening to sink the wealthy Catullus and his ship of precious cargo. 'Following the example of the Beaver, who makes a gelding of himself in the hope of saving his life at the sacrifice of sex', Catullus did not gamble his life for his fine fabrics and silver. 'Overboard with my possessions, over with them all!', he shouted, and thereby preserved his life at the expense of his cargo.[11] Cicero compared a man who left his wife behind while fleeing persecution to a beaver who saves his life by ransoming his most desired parts (the wife was raped by the husband's pursuers). If a hunter cornered a beaver who had already lost his testicles, the beaver was said to rear up on his hind legs or roll over onto his back to show the hunter he had nothing more to give. Aelian even suggested the beaver had a cunning streak: with 'great skill and ingenuity' beavers sometimes tucked up 'the coveted part', pretending they no longer possessed what they were concealing.[12]

A story will only endure for as long as it is worth telling. And certainly the fable of the beaver provided a wealth of agreeable untruths. The fable was simple and direct, yet ambiguous enough to serve a variety of lessons. (The only persistent interpretation through the centuries was that biting off your testicles was the principled thing to do.) It was bawdy – always a vote in any story's favour – yet at its core contained a solid and virtuous moral.

The beaver delighted early Christian moralists. Drawing on classic animal tales, medieval bestiaries converted ancient fables into parables illustrating key points of biblical doctrine. Animals were either good or bad and offered examples of the path towards salvation or sin. If ancient writers had stressed the beaver's prudence and common sense (why die for a few possessions?), early Christians fathomed a deeper spiritual truth. Beaver testicles came to symbolize all worldly possessions and fleshly wants. The hunter, interpreted as the devil, hounded the beaver mercilessly, just as sinners are hounded by their uncontrolled desires and lusts. Good Christians who wished to live chastely should follow the beaver, cut off all vices, and cast them to the devil.

For Christian interpreters, the moral truth of beast fables depended on divine benevolence: God so loved his followers that he infused the animal kingdom with a symbolic language by

The beaver from the *Medici Aesop*, a 15th-century manuscript of Aesop's fables, is a meek and demure creature.

which humankind's humble intelligence could be led towards a deeper understanding. The physical language of beasts spoke a transcendent significance. A practical god would put the industrious ant on earth to teach the lessons of hard work. But it takes a creator with a certain waggish imagination to give an animal sufficiently large teeth to neuter himself. And then to use the animal to teach the virtues of chastity is downright perverse. And in that sense, the tenacity of the fable through ancient poetry, Roman rhetoric and Christian texts had less to do with the obscurity of beaver biology than with the sublime absurdity of the fable itself. Once told, it is never forgotten.

But the tale has been forgotten. The ancient fabulist's other tales are among the best-known stories, having long passed into the realm of truisms and popular sayings. But while 'The Beaver and his Testicles' formed part of the classic canon of fables and continued to be included in most versions into the nineteenth century, Aesop's beaver is absent from modern editions. Certainly the tale became less appropriate when fables were re-imagined as children's stories. 'Safety should at times be bought with money',

A 13th-century carving on the cathedral of Sessa Aurunca in southern Italy depicts a beaver begging with hands folded in supplication. Perhaps he has met the hunter before.

'The Hunted Beaver', from a French edition (1802) of Francis Barlow's *Fables of Aesop; or, Aesopica*.

65

as Andrea Alciato put it in 1531, is not a lesson particularly suited to childhood education.[13] Nor is 'If you have had evil inclinations towards sin, greed, adultery, theft, cut them away from you and give them to the devil.'[14] Plus, the moral of the tale involved castration. Some books kept the tale but censored its graphic content. A version of the Fables printed in 1793 began with, 'It is said that a Beaver . . . has a certain part about him which is good in physic, and that, upon this account, he is often hunted down and killed.'[15] The omission kept the fable child-appropriate, but any curious mind would surely enquire what 'part' was implied. Then again, the fable may have vanished simply because it is untrue.

Admittedly, biological accuracy is hardly a prerequisite for fables, and Aesop was hardly a zoologist. Instead, the art of fabling beasts lies in capturing a truth of human nature as purified through the perfect simplicity of animal purpose. Classic tales such as 'The Wolf in Sheep's Clothing' or 'The Ant and the Grasshopper' infuse human intension through the animal world, elevating a behaviour such as hunting or hard work into a true-for-all-times-and-places sort of morality. Yet wolves are cunning hunters and ants are exemplary workers, and it is this kernel of animal wisdom that ultimately makes the fables' cautionary advice ring true. In contrast, 'The Beaver and his Testicles' is built on a series of bizarre biological falsehoods. Not a single part of the story is true – not castoreum's medicinal value, not its anatomical origins, not the beaver's self-sacrificing instinct. Nor was castoreum the reason beavers were so hotly pursued by hunters. By the seventeenth century, when naturalists finally exposed the fable's anatomical falsehoods, hundreds of thousands of North American beavers were being killed each year for their fur, not their scent.

The self-castrating beaver is just the first of many fetishized beavers that were cast aside when their merits became irrelevant or untenable. As we will see in the following chapters, representations of beavers are always fading or emerging, depending on which beaver part most fascinates and enthrals the mythmakers.

But we are not quite done with the musky beaver. As with many superior fragrances, beaver musk continued to intoxicate the human imagination long after the beaver itself had disappeared.

Castoreum has been used in perfumery for its warm and leathery scent. Often described as lustful, wild and bodily, beaver musk endowed perfumes such as Aramis by Estée Lauder, Magie Noire by Lancôme and Shalimar by Guerlain with their animalistic sensuality. On the palate, raw castoreum has a rank bitterness. But when diluted with alcohol, it develops a vanilla-like flavour and 'a warm, animal-sweet odor', according to *Fenaroli's Handbook of Flavor Ingredients*.[16] It adds a sweet, leathery taste to some cigarettes and has been used widely as a vanilla flavouring in baked goods, frozen dairy products, candy, puddings, non-alcoholic beverages and chewing gum. Real castoreum has mostly been replaced by a synthetic equivalent. However, any food product described as 'all natural' and containing 'natural vanilla flavour' (as opposed to vanilla) may contain castoreum, since the descriptor 'all natural' precludes any artificial ingredients. Also, the Federal Drug Administration estimates the daily intake per capita of castoreum is around 0.01261 milligrams – a minuscule amount, but not zero.[17]

Chemically speaking, castoreum is fascinating. Many plants have evolved toxic chemical defences to protect themselves against herbivores. The effects of such toxins range from mild digestive disruption to reproductive failure to outright death on consumption. In turn, herbivores have evolved ways to digest and cope with plants' defences. But beavers go one step better: beavers sequester the toxic compounds and biologically recycle them as castoreum, the animal's own liquid territorial defence system.

One of castoreum's more noteworthy compounds is salicylic acid, the active ingredient in aspirin, which is naturally found in the bark of willow trees. Castoreum also contains phenol from Scots pine (used in some oral analgesics for its anaesthetic properties), benzoic acid from black cherry (used medicinally for fungal skin diseases), catechol from common cottonwood (used as a pesticide and vanilla-like flavouring) and hydroquinone from red pine (used in photo developing and as a skin whitener).

The actual measure of therapeutic ingredients in castoreum is too small to cause either much good or harm. Besides, beaver musk was never prescribed for the sorts of general pain aspirin might alleviate. Rather, castoreum was long believed to be a powerful stimulant and antispasmodic. Pliny claimed it helped with vertigo, fits of trembling, flatulence, sciatica, stomachic complaints and epilepsy. Taken with vinegar it cured hiccups. When beaten with oil and injected into the ear, it cured a toothache on the same side. When mixed with hops and a teaspoon of water, it calmed palpitations of the heart. Hildegard von Bingen, an eleventh-century Benedictine abbess, suggested drinking castoreum with wine to check a fever. It was also said to neutralize the poisons of scorpion, spider and serpent bites and was one of the main ingredients in theriac, a near-mystical antivenom.

Castoreum was usually prescribed either as a powder or tincture. The powder was simply made by grinding up dried castor sacs. The basic *tinctura castorei* was prepared by steeping 60 g (2 oz) of bruised castor sacs in alcohol. After seven to fourteen days the sacs were removed, squeezed like tea bags and discarded, and the alcohol was filtered through paper. A more potent tincture was made by macerating 70 g (2½ oz) of castor sacs with 30 g (1 oz) of asafoetida (a stinking root from Afghanistan) in two pints of Spirit of Ammonia. Thirty to sixty drops was the usual recommendation.

. Castanee .

. Castoreum . alio noie asushthir

The ancient proof of castoreum's medicinal potency was its foetid aroma. Insinuating themselves into any orifice, above or below, smells were powerful treatments in the ancient world. Sweet perfumes or acrid stenches were used equally, variously to excite, tame or attract the body's fluids and spirits. For example, to open a closed and hardened womb, the ancient physician Hippocrates suggests fumigating the uterus with a potent smudge made of frankincense, wax, myrtle leaves, castoreum, lard and the excrement of a male ass. The Roman poet Lucretius included beaver musk in a list of vaporous toxins that 'slip up the nose, touch-textured, deadly stuff'.[18] On Mount Helicon grew a tree with flowers sufficiently foul-stinking to kill a man. Castoreum was far less lethal, but still, Lucretius observed that just a whiff caused menstruating women to fall abruptly into deep slumber. Pliny claimed that the vapours induced miscarriage – if a pregnant woman stepped over a jar of it or over a beaver itself, abortion would be the sure result.

Likely as not, castoreum's gynaecological virtues were believed to arise from its testicular origins. The ancient pharmacopeia literally bulged with highly suggestive ingredients reputed to help with ailments of the sexual parts. Gourds, horns, snakes, barley (ancient slang for pubic hair), myrtle (ancient slang for clitoris), dried animal penises, pomegranate, figs, squirting cucumbers, excrement and urine from bulls and other virile beasts were all regularly prescribed for sexual complaints. Interestingly, the beaver's supposed testicles were the only ones Hippocrates recommends in his broad corpus of medical treatments, and he prescribed them exclusively for ailments of women's sexual parts. Squat and lumbersome on land, the beaver is hardly the image of virility. One would have thought bull testicles or those from a stag would be far more potent. But then, the beaver's supposed testicles stank more than any other – a sure sign of their efficacy. And as ever, the more heady the fumes, the more dramatic the cure.

Castoreum was most widely prescribed for hysteria, a mysterious ailment encompassing a potpourri of symptoms: feelings of asphyxiation, violent fits, paralysis of the limbs and fainting. It exclusively afflicted women and supposedly arose from a toxic womb – the word hysteria is derived from the Greek word for uterus, *hystera*. One bizarre physiological theory held that a disgruntled womb would wander about the body, rising into a woman's chest, causing laboured breathing and the sensation of strangulation. Other theories suggested that symptoms were brought on by the retention and putrefaction of either sperm or menstrual blood. Following the traditional faith in scent therapy, the tenth-century Muslim physician Ibn al-Jazzar recommended anointing a woman's uterus with sweet-smelling oils while letting her sniff disagreeable smells like castoreum, tar, burned wool, and soot from an extinguished lamp. By such means, the corrupted fluids would recoil from the stench and, like an unruly beast, be drawn downwards towards the sweet aroma.

Victorian physicians continued to recommend castoreum, particularly for uterine disorders and hysteria. Any nineteenth-century medical manual will invariably list it among its pharmaceuticals. Some authors describe the various prescriptions and preparations but qualify them with 'in this country it is not much used', or some such caveat.[19] Other physicians simply dismissed castoreum along with the entire ancient tradition of insinuating smells. 'If articles of medicine are to be chosen from their powerful odour', one American physician mockingly writes, 'certainly we possess one superior to musk, to castor, and to the whole catalogue of antispasmodics. I mean the pole-cat or skunk.' Once stench lost its remedial powers, castoreum soon vanished from the pharmacopeia.[20]

Title page from
Moyse Charas'
treatise on the
composition of
theriac (Paris,
1668).

THERIAQVE
D'ANDROMACHVS
Par
Moyse Charas.

A PARIS Chez Oliuier de Varennes.

And finally, a word about castor oil. Despite its name, castor oil has nothing to do with beavers, nor was it a replacement for castoreum as is commonly supposed. Although castor oil is sometimes prescribed to induce labour, it was originally marketed as a powerful laxative for various bilious disorders, and castoreum was never prescribed for constipation. (Castor oil's alleged labour-inducing effects arise from its vigour on the bowels; violent abdominal cramps can sometimes start contractions.)

Castor oil comes from the seeds of *Ricinus communis*, a flowering shrub common throughout the Mediterranean, eastern Africa and tropical regions. The plant was well known in the ancient world; some authors claimed it was the tree under which Jonas rested after he was discharged from the whale. Ancient physicians frequently prescribed it for its purgative effects and called it *oleum ricini*, as *ricinus* is the Latin for tick, and the plant's ripe seeds resemble an engorged female tick, and *oleum* is the Latin for oil. (The biotoxin ricin is also derived from the castor oil plant.) The plant was also known as Palm of Christ for its palmated leaves and reputed healing powers.

The earliest use of the name 'castor oil' comes in a 1764 pamphlet published by Peter Canvane, who seems to have singlehandedly renamed the oil and brought it into common usage in Britain. According to Canvane, the plant grew widely on the Caribbean Islands, particularly on St Kitts where the oil was frequently used by both European physicians and the local inhabitants. As to its unlikely beaver name, Canvane suggested a strange multilingual distortion: the French inhabitants of St Kitts sometimes called the plant *agnus castus*, or chaste lamb,

> perhaps on account of the great efficacy of the oil in curing, and in temperating all *febrile* heats, and especially the heats of *venery*; from when, I suppose the people of St. Christophers,

who were formerly blended with the French in that island, have, by a corruption of *agnus castus*, called it *castor oil*.[21]

In the end, our romance with the musky beaver ends badly, at least for the beaver. For centuries, both castoreum and oil from its anal scent glands have been used against beavers as agents of death.

Although Heinrich Kuhl distinguished North American beavers as a separate species in 1820, and Frédéric Cuvier pointed out differences in the skulls in 1825, the two species were not conclusively proven until chromosomal testing in the 1970s. Unaware the two beavers were separate species, many early twentieth-century beaver reintroductions in Eastern Europe and Russia imported North American beavers in the hope of replenishing the Eurasian populations. The introductions were more than successful. The new beavers thrived. However, when the two beavers were positively confirmed to be separate species and unable to interbreed, biologists were faced with a serious problem. North American beavers were slightly more aggressive than their Eurasian cousins and had slightly larger families. Rather than bolstering a failing population, the introduced beavers were driving Eurasian beavers even closer to extinction. The new beavers were deemed invasive and required expunging. But how to tell one beaver from another? The two species were impossible to distinguish conclusively by sight alone, and a chromosomal test is hardly a handy field method.

In 1999 two scientists happened upon the simple but bizarrely improbable answer. Frank Rosell and Lixing Sun discovered that the secretions from beavers' anal scent glands vary in colour, scent and viscosity between species as well as between sexes. The secretions from North American males are sticky and brownish. Those of North American females are waterier and yellow with the strong smell of rancid fat. The secretions of Eurasian males

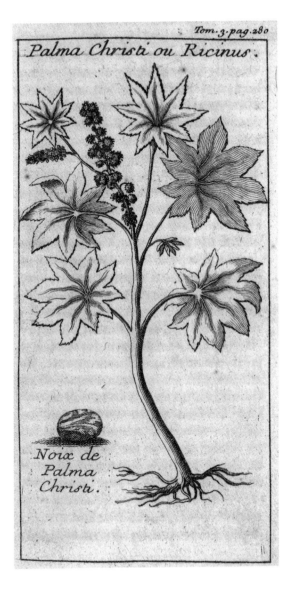

Tom. 3. pag. 280

Palma Christi ou Ricinus.

Noix de Palma Christi.

The castor bean plant, genus *Ricinus*, also known as 'palma Christi' or palm of Christ. From Jean-Baptiste Labat, *Nouveau voyage aux isles de l'Amerique* (1742).

are yellowish and watery while the females have extremely sticky, grey secretion with a distinct whiff of gasoline.[22] Oddly, the secretions of North American females closely resemble those of Eurasian males, which means if a beaver's smear is yellowish, the animal's sex must be confirmed by a ventral palpitation before its species can be determined.

Since glands can be milked from living beavers, the system offered a quick field method for scientists to identify which beavers were legitimate and which required expunging. As a further aid, Rosell and Sun matched the four secretions to the Pantone colour chart. (Scientists are now also training dogs to identify the invasive beavers by their scent.) The wrong hue of an anal smear may have caused the deaths of a few hundred beavers, but castoreum proved a far deadlier weapon against them.

Most early North American natural histories and travel narratives give detailed accounts of the best ways to trap and kill beavers. Since aboriginals were the main beaver hunters until the late eighteenth century, the texts usually describe traditional methods of breaking open dams, then netting or spearing the fleeing beavers. Sometimes the entrance to a lodge would be staked to prevent the animals from escaping. Sometimes dams were broken to lure beavers out for repairs.

Steel traps began replacing traditional methods by the late seventeenth century. Legend has it that aboriginal hunters, well acquainted with beavers' territoriality, were the first to bait their traps. According to Louis-Armand de Lom d'Arce, Baron de Lahontan, who travelled extensively through New France in the late seventeenth century, aboriginal hunters set their traps with red asp, a species of willow that beavers 'love extreamly, and is not easie to be found'. He also claimed traps were baited with the heads of otters, as beavers and otters were reputedly arch foes.[23] But asp twigs and otter heads were weak baits compared

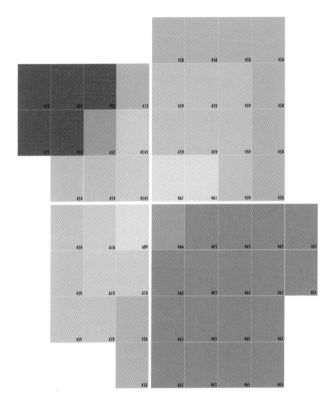

The Pantone colour chart of anal gland secretion specimens, as described by Frank Rosell and Lixing Sun in 'Use of Anal Gland Secretion to Distinguish the Two Beaver Species' (1999).

to the fail-safe beaver lure: castoreum from foreign beavers. Just a sprinkle was enough to draw wary beavers out from the water's safety to investigate and defend their property from suspected interlopers.

The earliest mention of castoreum-baited traps comes in the 1670s. The Anglican chaplain Charles Wolley claimed Algonquian-speaking people around New York anointed their traps with castoreum 'to allure and draw' beavers.[24] In 1728 William Byrd, a Virginian gentleman commissioned to survey the boundary

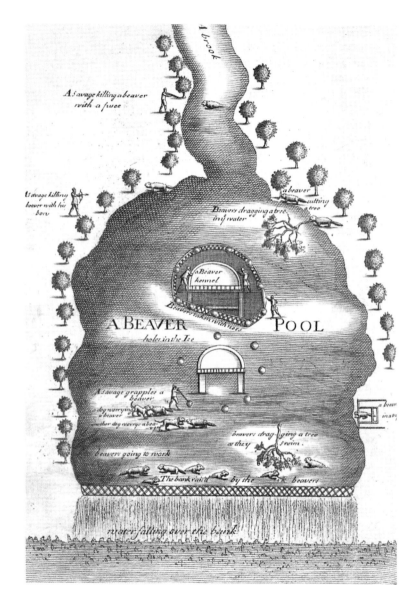

A brook

A ſavage killing a beaver
with a fuſee

A ſavage killing a
beaver with his
bow

a beaver
cutting
a tree

Beavers dragging a tree
in ſ water

a Beaver
kennel

Beavers taken with nets

A BEAVER   POOL

holes in the Ice

A ſavage grapples a
beaver

a dog worrying
a beaver

another dog worrys a bea-
ver

a beaver
in a trap

beavers drag-ging a tree
as they ſwim

beavers going to work

The bank raiſ'd   by the   beavers

water falling over the bank

line between Virginia and North Carolina, described a local English recipe of castoreum and sassafras bark. Another recipe described an intoxicating bait of castoreum, nutmeg, cloves and cinnamon stirred together with enough whiskey to give the consistency of mustard.[25] (Apparently the mixture could be kept in a corked vial for several months without losing potency.) Once steel traps baited with castoreum came into common usage, North American beaver populations were systematically obliterated from the Atlantic to the Pacific coasts.

The ancient fable of the self-castrating beaver was an old European myth about the Eurasian beaver. By the time New World beavers were discovered and the American fur trade began, the tale was an antiquated curiosity. 'It is besides a folly', the Jesuit priest Pierre François-Xavier de Charlevoix wrote in 1744, 'that when the beaver finds himself pursued, to save his life he bites off these pretended testicles.' 'It is his fur he ought then to strip himself of,' Charlevoix explained with a dark dose of reality, 'in comparison of which all the rest is of little value.'[26] As if the beaver had a choice.

Beaver trapping in North America, from Louis-Armand, Baron de Lahontan, *New Voyages to North-America* (1703).

3 Fur

I hope I may have a large beaver to-morrow.
John James Audubon, *Audubon and His Journals* (1897)

On 3 October 1686, Edward Newgent snatched the beaver hat and periwig off the head a London physician out for an evening stroll. Tucking the hat under his arm, Newgent made off at a run but was immediately apprehended. Being a repeat offender, he was found guilty and sentenced to death. On 25 April 1688, John Wyatt was tried for robbing a gentleman of his beaver hat. The gentleman took up the chase and seized Wyatt, who was also sentenced to death for highway robbery. And on 11 July of the same year, George Stockwell, a notorious shoplifter and pickpocket, was tried for stealing a beaver hat valued at 55 shillings from John Holmes, Esq. Holmes had bought the hat that afternoon and was travelling home by coach with the hat in its box beside him. Dark as the night was, Holmes saw the shadow of a hand reaching through the window, and suddenly the box was gone. Although the hat and its box were later found in the custody of Stockwell, he denied stealing them, and as the theft had occurred at night and Holmes could not positively identify the thief, Stockwell was acquitted.[1]

A gentleman's beaver hat was a luxury item in seventeenth-century England and could cost as much as £4 – about three months' wages for a low-skilled worker – making a high-quality beaver hat highly tempting for thieves and desperadoes. Between 1675 and 1700, 31 cases of snatched beaver hats were brought before

Francis Bacon: no matter the changing fashion, a beaver hat was the omnipresent accompaniment to every proper English gentleman until the mid-19th century.

the Old Bailey in London. By the end of the nineteenth century, no fewer than 222 beaver-related thefts had been tried. Most involved stolen hats – picked from heads or looted from wealthy residences, but raw materials also enticed thieves. According to the Old Bailey's records, in 1687 a Ms Cibile Jones was convicted, fined and branded for stealing four ounces of 'Rushia Beaver Wool', as the raw materials were known, and in 1722, the aptly named Henry Player tried his best to pilfer 80 skins from the Hudson's Bay Company, the fur monopoly which controlled much of the territory that is now Canada. Player had been crew on the frigate *Mary* as she made the Atlantic crossing, laden with North American furs. Crew members were forbidden to trade, so Player hid some furs in his cabin and some between the decks, and despite the testimony of abundant witnesses, somehow got away with it.[2] Beaver was as good as gold and as black as death. Of those 222 beaver thefts, twelve convicted thieves were whipped, 73 were transported to the New World and 45 were condemned to death. All for a hat.

Then again, a beaver hat was no ordinary thing. No matter the style, whether crowns rose or brims broadened, a beaver hat was in a class of its own. The trial of James Jordan and his midnight burglary of a haberdashery in 1688, for example, made careful distinction as to what sort of hats were involved. Jordan and his accomplices had taken two 'Beaver Hats' valued at £3, two 'Caster Hats' valued at 20 shillings, and eleven dozen 'Cordubeck Hats' valued at £44, or 7 shillings each. 'Beaver Hats' were the highest quality and were made from felted beaver wool, as beaver under-fur was known. Three times cheaper than beavers, 'Caster Hats', or castors, contained some beaver mixed with a higher percentage of inferior fur, such as hare or rabbit. And at a ninth of the cost of a beaver hat, a 'Cordubeck' likely contained no beaver at all. For his crime, Jordan was sentenced to 'Transportation' back across

the Atlantic, from whence the beaver had come. What happened to his accomplices is unknown.[3]

Of course, the most wretched victims of Europe's passion for beaver hats were the beavers themselves. No one knows quite how many beavers once roamed North America – estimates vary between 60 and 400 million – but for the better part of three centuries, tens of millions of beavers were steadily exterminated to make hats.

Beavers inhabited the river systems that acted as the main transportation network into the North American continent, which made them particularly easy to find. Their fixed abode, low

Two native hunters shoot ever-industrious beavers; a European turns his head away. From Claude Le Beau, *Avantures du Sr. C. Le Beau* (1738).

A trapper prepares to lower a beaver trap into a basin hole.

reproductive rate and late sexual maturity made beavers especially vulnerable to overhunting. Trappers often killed all the animals found in a lodge, kits included, and even trapped during the summer months, two wretchedly short-sighted practices that prevented beavers from reproducing. Once steel traps baited with castoreum became pervasive in the eighteenth century, the beaver was ruined. If extermination had been their objective, trappers could hardly have found more efficient means of eradication.

The first trading posts were established at Île de Sable in 1598 and at Tadoussac in 1600 on the Saint Lawrence River. Within a few decades, beavers were wiped from the region. On the eve of the American Revolution in 1775, beavers had been eradicated from the thirteen colonies. And by the early nineteenth century, beavers were on the brink of extinction in Canada's vast northern territories. For two centuries, traders simply pushed further and further west into the continent as beavers withdrew before them like a grimly receding hairline. But once trappers passed through the Rocky Mountains and reached the Pacific Ocean, there were no further beavers to discover.

The irony is that no one was looking for beavers. When Europeans first arrived at the coast of North America, they were driven by the same visions of gold, silver and spices that vitalized the exploration of South America. The oversized rodent barely makes an appearance in Jacques Cartier's reports from the Saint Lawrence River in the 1530s, although the region abounded in beavers. On his first voyage in 1534, a Mi'kmaq welcoming party approached in canoes holding up furs as a sign that they wanted to barter. But to Carter, they were 'the sorriest folk there can be in the world, and the whole lot of them had nothing above the value of five sous, their canoes and fishing-nets excepted'.[4] Furs were barely mentioned. Most early French accounts suggested the entire northeastern coast had little to offer. The land was fertile enough but its climate could only produce the same crops as were grown in Europe, which made it of limited agricultural value. There were no precious metals, or at least none readily available, no tropical fruits or hot spices. Moreover, the winters were long and breathtakingly harsh. On Cartier's second voyage, his crew wintered at the Iroquoian capital of Stadacona, near present-day Quebec. Although two degrees of latitude further south than Paris, Stadacona was buried under snow from mid-November until the end of April. The ships were locked in ice for six months, and the men were stricken with scurvy. Cartier heard rumours of a land to the north filled with gold and diamonds, but the gold turned out to be pyrite, and the diamonds were quartz. North America offered nothing to inspire colonization, let alone the effort of exploration.

It was the cod of the Grand Banks that brought Europeans back to North America – not to colonize or conquer but simply to fish – and it was European goods that brought local Algonquin, Montagnais and Hurons to the coastline to trade. In exchange for the highly desirable wares, particularly metal tools such as knives, axes and cooking pots, aboriginal traders brought furs, which were well received but not excessively so. Until the end of the sixteenth century no special missions were launched to trade furs. No trading posts were established. Europeans had known about the vast fur continent for more than half a century without making any effort to exploit it. And then, in 1581, Sweden captured the port city of Narva from the Russians. Within a few years Europe's deadly romance with North America's beaver was in full flush.

At the eastern edge of Estonia on the Baltic Sea, Narva was ideally situated at a trade crossroads. It was part of an ancient route connecting Scandinavia to Constantinople and, more importantly for the North American fur trade, European merchants with Russia's vast natural resources. A new middle class and commercial aristocracy were growing in Europe, and with increased prosperity came a desire for imported luxuries such as furs.

With the capture of Narva and Sweden's control of the Baltic, European traders were forced to sail all the way around Scandinavia in order to continue trading with Russia. Although the Dutch

The sumptuous commodities of the Americas on display.

established a new trading post at Archangel in 1585, and although Russians kept tariffs low to encourage trade, the westward wheels had already been set in motion. Besides, Russian beavers were in decline, which was pushing prices up.

As commodities, North American furs had several distinct advantages. There were no tariffs or taxes in the New World. Many fur-bearing animals were no longer found in Europe, a prime prerequisite to make overseas trade worthwhile. Furs were lightweight, non-perishable and easy to transport. And perhaps most importantly, they took minimal effort to acquire and very little expense to purchase. Native hunters were the ones who trapped and killed the animals, and sold them for what Europeans deemed mere trinkets.

Of course steel knives and cooking pots were hardly trinkets. Most aboriginals were in utter disbelief that such wares could be had for mere beaver. 'The English have no sense,' a Montagnais apparently joked to a French Jesuit missionary in 1634, they give us twenty knives like this one for one Beaver skin.' On both sides of the bargain, the humble beaver performed the extraordinary. It generated vast fortunes for Europeans, and for native trappers 'the Beaver does everything perfectly well, it makes kettles, hatchets, swords, knives, bread; and, in short, it makes everything'.[5] No group can be absolved from the devastation of the beaver. Aboriginal trappers, Hudson's Bay Company traders, the Mountain men of the upper Missouri, French Canadian *coureurs de bois* traversing the great northern rivers in their long canoes, middlemen, businessmen and of course the fashion-conscious consumers: all conspired to wipe out the beaver. Like an all-consuming fire, their burning passion blazed through the wilderness until there was hardly a beaver left.

Certainly, other fur-bearing animals were trapped and traded, but it is true enough to say that North America was built on the back of the beaver. Canada, in particular, was made by beaver. The Hudson's Bay Company was as good as its first government and its first tender was beaver skins, or 'made beaver', as the currency of pelts was known. Wars were waged over prime beaver territories. The Beaver Wars, King William's War and the French and Indian War were all beaver-driven, while the Treaty of Utrecht and the Louisiana Purchase were at least partially about access to

The West India Company rejected the proposed beaver coat of arms for New Amsterdam: lions were not sufficiently represented.

fur. Fur traders were always the first to push westward into the continent, and the first to meet and negotiate with aboriginal communities. (Some wag dubbed the Hudson's Bay Company 'Here Before Christ', sending up the fact that where trappers cut trails into the unknown, missionaries were quick to follow.) Beaver rewrote the relationships between aboriginal nations as well, with some establishing themselves as middlemen to capitalize on trade with Europeans. Although it was not the first time that furs had shaped empire – Russia's conquest of Siberia was driven in part by furs – the early North American trade was distinguished by its beaver focus. And while other furs were made into a variety of fashions, the beaver trade rested squarely on the stalwart superiority of beaver hats.

That much is a well-known story. What is less well known is how beaver hats came into existence and why they were so

Lor Par, are they Beavers? they aint a bit like your hat, you gave 2ˢ & 9ᵈ for, but I suppose they're more. waterproof!

extraordinarily popular. History books often claim it was Europe's rage for broad-brimmed hats that kicked off beaver mania in the seventeenth century, which is true. But the romance of fur is not quite so straightforward. Beaver hats were not simply beaver skins cut to shape and sewn together. Rather beaver hats were made from felted beaver underfur. As might be expected from a textile capable of founding nations and driving North America's early economic development, beaver felt is no ordinary material, and its invention was correspondingly remarkable. The dispersal of artisanal knowledge by ancient nomads, tightly held trade secrets, Dutch middlemen, a particular property of beaver underfur and just the right number of winter nights – an improbable collision of phenomena – conjoined to create an unparalleled all-weather hat that was worth a man's life.

An extraordinary number of processes were required to turn beaver fur into a beaver felt hat; *Eccentricities*, VII, c. 1840.

Or a woman's, for that matter. The fur trade and its nation-building history have traditionally been cast as masculine and patriarchal enterprises – a boy's beaver club, if you will – while landscapes are feminized and conquered. 'Canada', Chantal Nadeau explains, 'as the land of the beaver, owes its foundation to the penetration of the beaver trade/trail by European traders', by which she suggests an erotic geography of fur.[6] A beast, a pelt, a superlative hat, Canada's national symbol, and a euphemistic term for a woman's most personal anatomy, the beaver is jauntily cocked atop a kingdom of fur and its ever-shifting topography of fashion, fatalities and fortune.

Geoffrey Chaucer's merchant in *The Canterbury Tales* was a faddish man. He wore a colourful cloak, a forked beard, handsomely clasped boots, and 'on his hed a flaundrish bever hat'. The hat was Chaucer's key to the merchant's character: beaver hats were a distinguishing mark of rich fourteenth-century Flemings. To wear such a hat indicated that the merchant traded internationally and was part of a growing middle class with cosmopolitan sensibilities, or at least aspired to be.

What did a fourteenth-century flemish beaver hat look like? The Ellesmere manuscript suggests it had the jaunty cut of Errol Flynn's Robin Hood hat. Fifteenth-century images of merchants from Avignon also showed beaver hats as tight-fitting caps with long brims.[7] But European beavers were already scarce, and the trade in beaver hats was waning by the late medieval period. According to Marc Lescarbot's *Histoire de la Nouvelle-France*, published in Paris in 1609, beaver hats had only been back in use since 'the time of Jacques Cartier', although the French practice of making hats was not new. 'In the ancient privileges of the hat-makers of Paris, it is said that they are to make hats of fine beaver . . . but whether for the dearness or otherwise the use thereof had long since been left off.'[8]

Despite (or because of) the expense in the mid-sixteenth century, beaver hats were popular enough among the English aristocracy to be included in Philip Stubbes's *The Anatomie of Abuses*, first published in 1583. A Puritan pamphleteer and virulent crusader against whoredom, gluttony, drunkenness, gambling and other such vices as 'pestiferous Dauncing' and 'Football-playing on the Sabbath', Stubbes observed the prevalence of hats made of a certain kind of fine hair: 'These they call Bever hattes, of xx, xxx, or xl shillinges price, fetched from beyond the seas, from whence a greate sorte of other vanities doe come besides.'[9]

The theatrical fashions were certainly not unworthy of Stubbes's condemnation. Aristocratic gallants wore eccentrically tall hats, slightly tapered at the top with a narrow brim, known as sugar loaves. The style was probably inspired by the sheer expense of the materials required: these were vanity pieces and not to be worn on a windy day. A self-portrait of Isaac Oliver (who would become a portraitist for King James I) from around 1590 shows a dapper

Marianne Corless, *Fur Queen II*, 2001. A portrait of Elizabeth II, made in fur of mink, muskrat, beaver and ermine.

young man with a frothy ruff and a comically tall beaver hat. A portrait of King James VI of Scotland, a known dandy, exhibits an even taller hat, more rakishly narrow, perched on the very top of his head. And when James also became King James I of England in 1603, he ordered twenty beaver hats, seventeen of which were to be black, lined with taffeta and trimmed with black bands and feathers.[10] Perhaps those twenty hats were made from North American beaver.

By the turn of the century, the fur trade was proving sufficiently profitable that governments began to take an interest.

Trade monopolies were granted, usually on the condition that companies establish colonies to solidify their nation's territorial ambitions, but the region's harsh climate offered few pleasures to would-be colonists. France tried and failed to establish colonies at Île de Sable and Tadoussac, and in 1604 founded Acadia, which also foundered in 1607, the same year English traders built a fort at Jamestown. In 1613, London feltmakers and hatters lobbied Parliament to ban the importation of foreign-made hats, which suggests the London industry was well in swing. (In 1660 Parliament replaced the ban with a more financially advantageous tariff of 9 shillings and sixpence on imported beaver hats that steadily rose to 51 shillings by 1784.) Certainly by the time Samuel de Champlain founded Quebec in 1608, North America's fur trade had decidedly shifted from a seasonal coastal traffic into what Glynnis Hood aptly termed 'a mammalian gold rush'.[11] 1608 was also the year the Dutch East India Company launched their first ships westward. They established New Amsterdam (renamed New York in 1665 after it was ceded to the English) and quickly developed 'a handsome considerable peltry trade that can be assessed at several tons of gold annually',[12] as Dutch colonist Adriaen van der Donck observed in 1655. And perhaps most famously of all, in 1620 the Pilgrims crossed the Atlantic Ocean on the *Mayflower*, established Plymouth Colony and began repaying their debts with beaver pelts. It goes without saying that the Pilgrims' iconic tall-crowned hats were made with beaver.

That the Pilgrims wore tall felt hats, a sort of simplified sugar loaf, suggests the speed with which North American beaver pelts transformed European millinery and brought beaver hats into an ever-widening circle of consumers. Admittedly, the Pilgrims had lived in Amsterdam and Leiden since 1607, where beaver hats were more affordable than anywhere else in Europe. At the

King James VI wearing a precariously tall beaver hat, c. 1590.

Jan Solomonsz. de Bray, *The Regents of the Children's Almshouse in Haarlem*, 1663. The gentlemen wear the modified sugar loaves made famous by the Pilgrims of Plymouth Colony.

centre of a global trade network, Amsterdam flourished in the seventeenth century, and beaver hat styles mushroomed with the city's growing wealth. The voluminous hats depicted in so many paintings by Johannes Vermeer, Rembrandt van Rijn and other Dutch masters were all made from beaver. By the 1630s the vogue was broad brims and slouched crowns, often decorated with a jaunty white feather. Broad-brims were also worn by fashionable women, many of whom adopted a distinctly masculine style of dress. But hats were not only about style: they flaunted class, wealth, and also spoke an allegiance. The wide-brimmed slouch originated among Swedish cavaliers. With Sweden's rise to power during the Thirty Years War, the style spread through northern

Europe, particularly among fellow Protestant countries. And of course they were all made of beaver.

How do we know the hats were made from beaver? Fashion may be swayed by any number of influences, but the passion for beaver hats was not driven by the visual appeal of felted beaver underfur – all felt looks more or less the same, especially when dyed. Rather, beaver styles were inspired by the sheer possibilities of the material.

Most furry animals have two kinds of fur: long and silky guard hairs protecting a shorter, denser underfur. Furs are classified as fancy or staple, depending on which part of the pelt is most valued by furriers. Fancy furs such as mink, sable and fox are

Officers wear the wide-brimmed cavalier hat, in an era when hats spoke of political allegiance. Hendrik Gerritsz. Pot, *The Officers of the St Adrian Militia Company in 1630*, 1630.

admired for the lustrous colour and softness of their guard hairs. The fur is left on the pelt and sewn into garments or trim. In contrast, staple furs are most valued for their woolly underfur, which is cut from the pelt and felted. Through a process of applying heat, moisture, agitation and pressure, felted fibres become permanently entangled, creating a dense matt that will not unravel and can be moulded into shapes without seams.

Felt can be made from most animal fibres, but beaver underfur has a unique property which makes beaver felt unsurpassed in strength and endurance: each hair of underfur is covered with dozens of microscopic barbs. During the felting process, the barbs mesh together so firmly that beaver felt is able to withstand all manner of inclement weather. While cloth or goat felt hats slouch over time, beaver hats hold their shape after years of hard wear. Beaver felt does not tear or unravel. It is waterproof, supple enough to mould into any shape, and smoother than chamois leather. Beaver felt was the only material capable of supporting wide and durable brims, and such shape-holding resilience ensured that until the early nineteenth century, whether styles broadened or rose, grew pointed or cornered, any tall, large or crisply shaped hat could only be made from beaver.

The sugar loaf, the swag of the cavalier's chapeau, the three-cornered Tricorne, the uncocked colonial, the voluptuous ladies' Gainsborough hat bedecked with lavish plumes and ribbons, and an exaggerated curved chapeau known as L'Androsmane, were all made from beaver felt, as was the top hat, which ascended as the only suitable headgear for gentlemen. The bicorns famously worn by Napoleon Bonaparte and Horatio Nelson were of course necessarily beaver; a naval officer in particular required a hat that could withstand freezing and salty winds without an embarrassing droop. Before rubber, before Gore-Tex, there was beaver. Europe's infatuation is understandable, but the popularity of

Thomas Gainsborough's portrait of Georgiana Cavendish, Duchess of Devonshire, launched the popularity of the wide-brimmed Gainsborough hat among aristocratic beauties.

beaver hats does not explain beaver felt's unlikely invention. Whoever decided to felt a beaver, and why?

The discovery of felt is usually attributed to Central Asia. Prehistoric nomads combed and boiled the hair of their goats and sheep to make felt for tents, shoes and hats. The earliest archaeological evidence of felt dates to 6500 BC and is found in

Napoleon's beaver bicorne, abandoned at the Battle of Waterloo, on display at the German Historical Museum, Berlin.

the remains of the Neolithic town of Çatalhöyük in Turkey. Until at least the flourishing of the Graeco-Roman Empire, Turkey had a healthy beaver population, but surely no herdsman bothered to trap, kill and make felt from wild Turkish beavers when tame goats and other domestic animals could be easily brushed. Besides, even if some craftsmen had taken the time and effort to felt beaver, they would hardly have benefited from or even realized what made beaver felt extraordinary. It was only when the knowledge of felt-making migrated into northern geographies that the inherent superiority of beaver felt was discovered and appreciated. The same camel-felt hat that looks so crisp under a southern sun slumped into a sodden mass when buffeted and soaked by the winds and rains of northern winters.

Interestingly, early evidence of felt is also found in Russia's mountainous Altai Republic. Heavily forested with 60,000 km

(37,000 miles) of waterways, 7,000 lakes and average January temperatures dipping between −9°C (16°F) and −31°C (−24°F), the region is built for beavers, which means it is also built for the benefits of beaver hats. Situated dead centre in Asia, bordering Mongolia's deserts and the Siberian taiga, Altai sits at the perfect crossroads for southern felt to meet northern winters. If knowledge of felting did spread northwards from Turkey into Altai, the region may well be the birthplace of the felted beaver hat. Perhaps beavers were killed for their meat (often described as having the flavour of mutton with a fishy aftertaste), and then some experimental hunters made use of the animal's fur.

But still it seems wildly improbable that anyone ever discovered beaver felt's extraordinary powers. In contrast to sheep or

The trade in second-hand beaver hats was a booming business.

THE PAWNBROKERS SHOP.

goat hair, which can be simply combed from a living animal and felted, beaver fur requires two further procedures to felt. Beaver underfur must first be separated from the guard hairs before the fur will felt. Furthermore, the smooth keratin surface of each hair must be abraded, but not damaged, to raise each hair's barbs and release the superior meshing power of beaver underfur.

When those procedures were discovered is lost to time, but once discovered, they became a trade secret carefully guarded by Russian furriers. Moreover, Russians had developed a technique whereby underfur could be combed from the pelts, leaving the silky chestnut-brown guard hairs intact. The pelts could then be used as fancy furs by the garment industry, thereby doubling beavers' profitability.

It makes sense that Russia, one of the last beaver outposts in Eurasia, had the corner on the medieval beaver-wool trade. A durable and waterproof hat would be particularly appealing during a long, cold, snow-blown Russian winter. But, equally importantly, those cold Russian winters ensured that Russian beavers made better felt than most European beavers, which is to say that although beaver underfur was in a class of its own, not all beavers were created equal. Animals living in colder climates have denser underfur, and the densest underfur produces vastly superior felt. Even if the ancient inhabitants of Çatalhöyük had made felt hats from their Turkish beavers, they would have been poor cousins to a hat made from the winter fur of Russian beavers.

Because Russian furriers held the secret of turning beaver pelts into beaver wool, even after the discovery of North American beavers European hatters continued to import their beaver wool from Russia – except the wool was from North American beavers. The long and bizarrely circuitous route travelled by pelts, and the effort and expense traders, furriers and hatters endured to turn those pelts into a hat, only underscores the remarkable and unparalleled properties of beaver felt.

From the beginning of the fur trade until the later eighteenth century, the typical route from beaver to hat usually began with French and English traders purchasing pelts from aboriginal trappers, who might have already travelled long distances, perhaps trading the furs from other communities. European traders then transported furs across the Atlantic and sold them to Dutch middlemen, who shipped the pelts to Russia. Once Russian furriers had combed out the underfur, they sold it back to Dutch merchants, who in turn sold it mostly to French and English hatters.

The main products sent to Russia were skins stretched and dried on hooped branches known as *castor sec*, or dry beaver. *Castor sec* was named in distinction to *castor gras*, or greasy beaver, which were beaver skins unpicked from aboriginals' winter robes. Improbably, those winter robes were one of the crucial and most lucrative components of the fur trade.

The robes were made with six or seven beaver pelts, which were scraped clean of flesh, rubbed with animal marrow, trimmed and sewn together with sinew. Scraping the skin loosened the guard hairs' deep roots, and because robes were worn fur side in, the sweat, heat and friction of skin against fur worked the guard hairs loose and broke down the underfur's keratin coating. After a year of wear, the guard hairs were mostly gone, and furriers only needed to cut the fuzzed underfur from pelts. Good beaver felt was made with a mixture of *castor gras* and *castor sec*, and because *castor gras* did not need to be sent to Russia, beaver robes were furry bullion.

Those unbearably cold winters that Cartier endured not only endowed Canadian beavers with exceptional fur but were also the environmental impetus for warm beaver robes. Nations from southerly latitudes had no need of winter robes, which meant

A beaver pelt stretched on a hooped branch to dry.

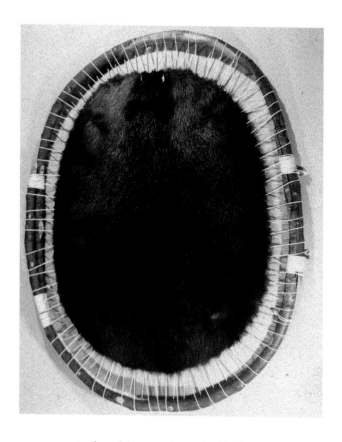

easy access to the coldest terrain was highly financially advantageous. When the Hudson's Bay Company first began trading in northern Canada, they expedited delivery by sailing their large ocean-worthy ships right into Hudson's Bay and literally purchased the robes off the backs of aboriginal traders. For the only time in the history of the fur trade, *castor gras* flooded the market. To manage the oversupply, the Company trialled a new product: beaver stockings. The fashion did not catch on.

However, for most of the fur trade *castor sec* was wildly over-produced. Surely one of the saddest facts in the long litany of beaver calamities is that millions of pelts rotted unused because the beavers had not endured sufficiently cold winters. Beavers were found as far south as California and Nevada. In fact, once American traders pushed through the Rocky Mountains, a veritable beaver gold rush hit New Mexico in the early nineteenth century. Without long winters, the underfur of southern beavers was too thin to make high-quality felt. But that hardly stopped the beaver fever. New Mexican beavers were all but extinct within a few decades. The summer coats of northern Canadian beavers were likewise thin and worthless, but sheer greed and ignorance

Dried beaver skins.

compelled trappers to kill beavers year round. The greed for beavers reached such heights that supply doubled over demand, and skins often sat mouldering in warehouses in the hope of raising prices. But still trapping continued. The fur trade was the lifeblood of North America. Too many livelihoods depended on a steady supply of beaver and the promise of wealth was too great. Trappers, traders and businessmen could not simply stop, until the beaver finally collapsed.

In a way, beavers got a small revenge. In the late seventeenth century, English hatters discovered a way of opening the underfur's barbs, thereby avoiding the cost of Dutch and Russian middlemen. Commonly known as carroting (it tinted pelts orange),

Along with the occupational hazards of hatmaking, Lewis Carroll's iconic Mad Hatter may have been inspired by the eccentric furniture dealer Theophilus Carter.

the toxic process of soaking pelts in salts of mercury and nitric acid revolutionized the English hat trade. In 1700 England exported 69,500 beaver hats. Within 60 years that number had risen to half a million, and from 1700 to 1770, 21 million beaver hats were exported from England.[13] As with all such highly profitable trade secrets, carroting's early history is shrouded in mystery. One theory holds that French Huguenot hatters brought the knowledge to London when they fled religious persecution. Another legend claimed that a doctor, attempting to cure a patient's breast cancer, made a beaver-pelt poultice spread with mercury. The pelt was discovered in a bin by a furrier, who recognized that mercury had broken down the keratin.[14] But no matter its origin, the process had deathly consequences. Labouring over hot mercury-soaked skins and breathing in the fumes resulted in a neurological deterioration commonly known as Mad Hatter Syndrome. Prolonged exposure to mercury vapours caused jerky tremors, pathological shyness and irritability, which explains at least in part Alice's odd encounter with the Hatter in Wonderland.

With a deadly hatter's disease, we reach the final reckoning of the beaver trade. By the early decades of the nineteenth century, silk was replacing beaver in gentlemen's top hats. While vacationing in France, the ever-shrewd John Jacob Astor foresaw the end. Astor founded the American Fur Company in 1808 and quickly made himself into the richest man in the world and America's first multimillionaire. But by 1832, beaver was out of vogue in Paris: 'I very much fear beaver will not sell well soon unless it is very fine', Astor wrote to a friend. 'It appears that they make their hats of silk in place of beaver.'[15] Astor sold his company two year later, and within a decade the fur trade collapsed. Along with the popularity of smooth silk, beaver populations were destroyed, and cheaper nutria fur was beginning to take a market share. It is surely an indication of the depressed value of beaver hats that

The decorative beaver tiles adorning Astor Place subway station in New York City are a nod to the making of the millionaire.

by 1847 it was the thief, and not his victim, who wore 'a beaver hat, a sort of plaid shooting-coat, and drab boots'.[16]

The fur trade has never died – beaver pelts are sold for about $20 and the quality of Stetson hats are still determined by their percentage of beaver fur. But the vocabulary of a beaver trade has morphed into something altogether different. For centuries 'beaver' was synonymous with a high-quality hat, but hats are no longer commonly worn. Seeing a beaver on the street has come to mean something quite different, which brings us at last to the delicate issue of the beaver 'down below'.

'Johnny, Cock Up Thy Beaver' was first printed in the seventh edition of John Playford's wildly popular *The Dancing Master*, published in 1686, the same year poor Edward Newgent was condemned to death for stealing a beaver hat. The origins of the jig are obscure, but the song likely satirizes a Scottish bumpkin who came down to England and adopted the latest fashions. A century later, Robert Burns wrote his own version, simply titled 'Cock up Your Beaver', which poked fun at the English:

> When first my brave Johnie lad came to this town,
> He had a blue bonnet that wanted the crown;
> But now he has gotten a hat and a feather,
> Hey, brave Johnie lad, cock up your beaver![17]

Johnie's blue bonnet was likely a woollen cap which wanted a crown because it sagged. To 'cock up your beaver' meant to turn the front brim of one's beaver hat up or set it at a jaunty angle. But all such explanations are needless. 'Cock up your beaver' has come to suggest something too vulgar for most listeners to bother with what Burns actually meant. And while 'fur', 'fur patch' and 'pelt' have all been sexualized, surely 'beaver' is the queen of all fur slang referring to a woman's pubic area. Saying 'beaver' invariably produces a snigger, and it hardly needs to be cocked.

As might be expected, rumours circulate around the term's origins. One theory rests on the fact that both beaver pelts and syphilis were imported from North America. According to legend, prostitutes who contracted syphilis designed themselves merkins of silky beaver fur to hide the disease's unsightly evidence. Thereby the New World provided both the curse and cover-all.

But the slang seems to have evolved much later, likely in the early twentieth century, as a sly slip downwards from the masculine beard above. As beards became fashionable in the

1920s (influenced in no small part by Vladimir Lenin and the Bolshevik revolution), a cheeky street game developed known simply as 'Beaver'. Scored like tennis, the game was played by two persons, who shouted 'beaver!' if they saw a bearded man. In 1922, John Kettelwell published a droll instructional handbook containing an alphabet of beavers with illustrations of 26 beaver specimens including the Admiral beaver, the Mandarin beaver, the Licked beaver (an almost extinct species distinguished by a slick spear-form on the chin), the Nanny beaver (a narrow chin beaver 'reported to flourish in the Eastern farming states of the United States of America') and the Queen beaver (a woman with a minimum of sixteen hairs on her chin). A double-fault results when a competitor thinks he sees a bearded man from behind, but when the two come face-to-face the competitor finds he is mistaken. Lampchops were usually to blame.

The game seems to have originated to mock the well-established beards of Oxford dons, which perhaps got their beaver name from the aquamarine beaver in Oxford's coat of arms. (To be 'in beaver' was also a slang term for non-academic attire; to wear a beaver hat rather than the academic cap and gown.) Aldous Huxley, who studied English literature at Oxford, was certainly familiar with the game. 'Beaver!' is frequently hollered in his 1923 dystopian sex farce *Antic Hay*. To overcome his shyness with women, one of the main characters, Theodore Gumbril, concocts himself a manly disguise. The disguise revolves around a pair of pneumatic trousers and a false beard, fan-shaped and blond, which he adheres with spirit gum. His mild and melancholic persona vanishes into jovial confidence, like 'a sheep in beaver's clothing'. Dressed in 'The Complete Man', as he dubs his disguise, Gumbril sidles up to a young lady in a store and says, 'If you want to say Beaver . . . you may.'[18]

Street 'Beaver' remained popular enough to make an appearance in George Stevens's 1942 comedy *The Talk of the Town*, starring

According to John Kettelwell, the best locales for spotting beavers were cathedral cities, Pall Mall and dockyards.

BEAVER

An Alphabet of typical Specimens with 26 Illustrations, together with Notes and a terminal Essay on the manners and customs of Beavering Men

A magnificent Specimen of the Bald-King Beaver in full winter coat.

1/-

JOHN KETTELWELL

L is for Licked Beaver, a very rare species generally regarded as extinct.

BEAVER

Cary Grant, Jean Arthur and Ronald Colman. Colman plays Professor Lightcap, whose beard is one of the film's running jokes. Lightcap grew the beard to cultivate an impression of gravitas, but it only provokes amusement. At one point, two strolling schoolgirls point to Lightcap and call out 'Beaver!', which by 1942 most certainly had a bawdy pleasure about it. According to the *Oxford English Dictionary*, the earliest printed use of 'beaver' for the region down below comes in a lewd limerick printed in 1927. Limerick LIV in the anonymously published *Immortalia: An Anthology of American Ballads, Sailors' Songs, Cowboy Songs, College Songs, Parodies, Limericks, and Other Humorous Verses and Doggerel* goes like this:

> There was a young lady named Eva
> Who filled up the bath to receive her.
> She took off her clothes
> From her head to her toes,
> And a voice at the keyhole yelled, 'Beaver!'[19]

That exclamation of 'Beaver!' clearly references the beard-spotting street game and suggests the sexual slang was a cunning comparison between a man's beard above and a woman's beard below. (The term 'bearded clam' backs up that theory.) Huxley also insinuates sexual innuendos were afoot; calling out beaver beards is far too funny for something lewd not to be involved. When the hedonist Coleman first makes his appearance in *Antic Hay*, he offers an irreverent ditty to explain his new beard:

The beaver supporter in Oxford's coat of arms may refer to the River Thames, although a beaver and an elephant both appear in the arms of a family associated with the city's history.

> Christ-like in my behaviour,
> Like every good believer,
> I imitate the Saviour,
> And cultivate a beaver.[20]

But Coleman had a double entendre in mind: 'There are some beavers', Coleman continues, 'which were so born from their mother's womb.' Thereupon he bursts into a fit of outrageous laughter. 'Hideous,' his friend Lypiatt sighs, 'hideous.'[21]

Meanwhile, the double meaning of 'beard' stretched back at least to the sixteenth century. A story from *A Hundred Merry Tales* (1526) has a woman and a young lad engaged in ribald repartee. The woman comments on the youth's beard, which has not yet filled in, growing luxuriously on his lip but sparse on his chin. 'Sir', she says, 'ye have a beard above and none beneath', which he counters with, 'Mistress, ye have a beard beneath and none above.' But the lady is not to be outdone. 'Marry', she retorts, 'then set the one against the t'other', suggesting their two half beards, when joined, would form one luxurious patch.[22] In a similar vein, the 1796 edition of *A Classical Dictionary of the Vulgar Tongue* defines

114

'beard splitter' as 'a man much given to wenching'.[23] From beard to beaver to beard again, the longevity of the sexual slang is surely sustained by the wonderfully lewd truth that beavers are wet, hairy animals that eat wood. That the dumpy beaver is hardly a vision of erotic animal nature only heightens the amusement.

The joke never ends in Canada. Canada has always been beaver country, all puns intended. Moose, loons, polar bears and caribou are national icons, but beavers embody Canada, and stuffed beavers can be found in almost every museum, park and nature education centre across the country.

The Canadian icon and female genitalia have never come together so intimately as in Wendy Coburn's *The Spirit of Canada Eating Beaver*, a bronze sculpture of a reclining nude woman with a beaver at work between her legs. The sculpture is an eroticized and modernized reference to Joyce Wieland's famous sculpture *The Spirit of Canada Suckles the French and English Beavers*, in which Canada, depicted as a reclining nude, nurses two plump little beavers.

Wieland's sculpture was part of her 1971 show *True Patriot Love*, the first major exhibition at the National Gallery of Canada given to a living Canadian female artist. Wieland developed a distinctly feminized patriotism for Canada that unravelled the myth of the Founding Fathers while also speaking to fears for national unity between French- and English-speaking Canadians. (Terrorist acts by French-Canadian separatists in 1970 led to the prime minister invoking the War Measures Act.) By reworking the legend of Rome's twin founders, Romulus and Remus, who were saved and suckled by a she-wolf, Wieland feminized the nation as an all-giving, all-loving mother who simultaneously and without bias nourished both French and English Canada.

Three decades later, Coburn's *The Spirit of Canada Eating Beaver* sidesteps the sovereignty debates between French and English

Jin-me Yoon, *Souvenirs of the Self (Banff Park Museum)*, from the series *Souvenirs of the Self*, 1991–2001. Searching for Canadian identity in stuffed symbolism.

Canada and transcends the feministic critic of the Founding Fathers. By eroticizing Wieland's maternal image, Coburn celebrates 'a homoerotic non-procreative sex which salutes one of the nation's earliest commodities and oddest amphibious rodents'. Time-worn national debates fall away into sensuality. The currency of beaver pelts was once as good as gold. But 'to women who "do" women', as Coburn puts it, the beaver's cultural currency 'is pure pleasure'.[24]

The beaver has always been an over-determined metaphor for human sexuality. Aesop claimed beavers castrated them-selves. Hippocrates prescribed beaver testicles for disgruntled wombs. From masculine beards to female genitalia, beavers have been the centre of highly gendered imaginings. But the anatom-ical truth of beavers is quite the reverse. Not only do male and female beavers look identical (ventral palpitation is required to determine the presence of a baculum), it is not uncommon for male beavers to have a uterus – a non-functioning masculine uterus that typifies a mammalian condition called intersexuality. This

Wendy Coburn, *The Spirit of Canada Eating Beaver*, 1999–2000, bronze.

117

pseudo-hermaphrodism does not affect the beaver's reproductive ability and only further accentuates the animal's egalitarian nature. For all the sexual talk, male and female beavers are virtually identical, work amicably side-by-side at the same tasks, and are all androgynous.

Yet the euphemistic beaver has caused Canada's oldest magazine to change its name. Founded in 1920 to commemorate the Hudson's Bay Company's 250th anniversary, *The Beaver* originated as a company newsletter with general circulation beginning in 1923. The magazine was dedicated to exploring Canadian history, and the name was a nod to the animal's foundational importance to the company and the nation. But by the 1990s, the name was increasingly problematic. In an issue from 1995, the editor wrote, 'Unfortunately, there are some people who come to the conclusion that it must be some sort of pornographic magazine or a periodical for nudists.' Others insisted on sending in 'rude photographs and clippings, which once caused consternation at the front desk and are now consigned to the trash bin with a yawn and a groan. It is a boring old joke by now.'[25] In the hope of clarifying the exact nature of the magazine, *The Beaver* acquired the subtitle, 'Exploring Canada's History'. But then the Internet age arrived. The magazine was lost in cyber pornography, and its online material was blocked by spam filters. In 2010, *The Beaver* became *Canada's History*.

Even before Canada existed (confederacy was not until 1867), the beaver was Canada's mascot. Canada's first stamp, issued in 1851, proudly displayed a beaver, making it the first animal ever to grace an official stamp. In 1937 a beaver appeared on Canada's nickel where it still remains, and in 1975 the rodent became the official symbol of Canada's sovereignty. Political cartoons invariably portray Canada as a beaver, with no captions or explanations required. Beavers adorn the Canadian Parliament Buildings in

A Second World War propaganda poster featuring a Canadian beaver gnawing away at the tree in which Adolf Hitler is hiding.

GET YOUR TEETH
INTO THE
JOB

Issued by the DIRECTOR OF PUBLIC INFORMATION UNDER AUTHORITY OF HON. J. T. THORSON, MINISTER OF NATIONAL WAR SERVICES, OTTAWA. Printed in Canada. UE-05

Kari Rust, *Stuffed Beaver, 70 Mile House*, 2001. Pledge your allegiance to Canada's beaver.

the nation's capital. But if the four beavers in the Hudson's Bay Company's coat of arms were symbols of the animal's economic importance to the country, beavers have come to embody, once again, something altogether different.

At precisely the moment beavers were slaughtered by the hundreds of thousands to make felt hats, those same beavers ascended as the supreme animal model of hard work, integrity and perseverance. The industrious beaver began to gnaw during the eighteenth century and has never stopped. Endowed with an ever-willing, ever-ready work ethic, beavers became synonymous with busyness. For a while, beaver hats and beaver industry co-existed, but with the collapse of the fur trade, the busier beaver summarily dispatched its hoary precursor. As the English novelist William Kingston put it in 1884, 'The beaver has fitly been selected as the representative animal of Canada, on account of its industry, perseverance, and hardihood, and the resolute way in which it overcomes difficulty.'[26]

Was this an attempt to create a new national imaginary, to excuse the millions of dead beavers that birthed Canada by lauding the animal's resilience? Perhaps. Certainly in 1884 no one could have predicted beavers' astonishing fortitude as they rebounded from the brink of extinction. And as we shift from beaver fashions to beaver industry, from animal product to animal agent, the work ethic and determination of living beavers – the 'busy beaver' of popular parlance – finally makes an appearance, although the next chapter hardly moves us any closer to the 'real' beaver, whichever animal that might be.

Plate XII

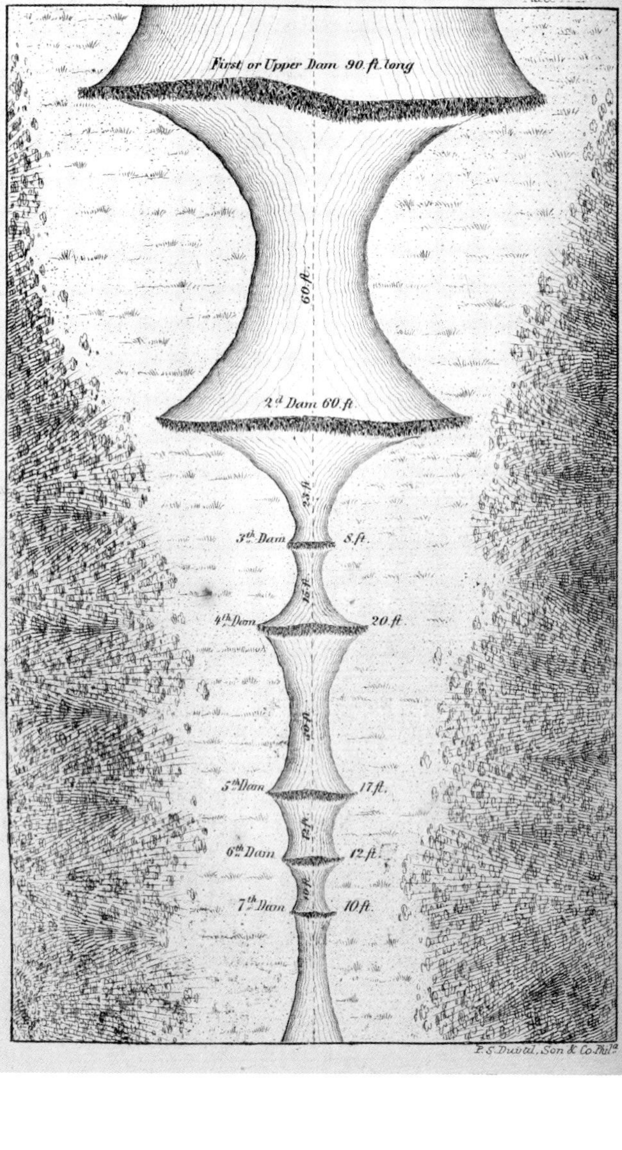
First or Upper Dam 90 ft. long
60 ft.
2d Dam 60 ft.
25 ft.
3th Dam
8 ft.
15 ft.
4th Dam
20 ft.
30 ft.
5th Dam
17 ft.
12 ft.
6th Dam
12 ft.
10 ft.
7th Dam
10 ft.

P. S. Duval, Son & Co. Phil.

4 Architect

Let us hear no more of the half-reasoning elephant; he is but a ninny to the beaver of America.

Frances Thurtle Jamieson, *Popular Voyages and Travels throughout the Continents and Islands of Asia, Africa, and America* (1820)

The Haida Nation of the Haida Gwaii archipelago off the Pacific Northwest coast of British Columbia has a story of a young woman who married a great hunter. She travelled with him to new hunting grounds in a lonely country away from her people. They built a home together in the wilderness and were happy. One day, the hunter set off to hunt and stayed away for two nights. His next hunt took him further into the forest, and he stayed away for a week. To amuse herself, the woman swam in the little stream and pond by their cabin. Soon the pond grew too small for her, so she built a dam by piling up branches and mud across the stream. She began spending all her days in the lake and even built a sleeping lodge in the middle of the water. The next time the hunter left, she was pregnant. To pass the time she raised the dam and built another dam downstream and another until she had several connecting ponds. The water rose to cover the entrance of her lodge.

When the hunter finally returned he could not find his wife. He searched the woods for many days, fearful some animal had eaten her. One evening at dusk, as he sat by the lake crying and singing a dirge for his wife, a strange animal with a stick in its mouth emerged from the water with two smaller animals also gnawing sticks. 'Do not be sad', the animal said, 'it is I, your wife, and your two children. We have returned to our home in the

A series of beaver dams from Lewis Henry Morgan's *The American Beaver and His Works* (1868).

123

water.' Her long hair had become her fur, and her leather apron had transformed into a beaver tail. She told her husband to go back to his people and to use her as his crest. 'I will be known as Woman-Beaver. The crest shall be called Remnants-of-Chewing-Stick. The children are the first Beaver, and you will refer to them in your dirge as the Offspring-of-Woman-Beaver.' And then Woman-Beaver returned to the water, and the hunter saw her no more.[1]

The legend gives voice to all that is captivatingly human and implausibly true about beavers; there is something uncannily recognizable in their habits, something familiar and knowable in their ways of managing life, family and home. For wild animals, beavers are highly domestic. They build and maintain a homestead while keeping an ever-watchful eye on the water level to ensure a safe and pleasing existence for their families. And although we know intellectually that beavers honed their architectural skills over millions of years, the Haida legend offers an origin story which, in its own way, makes just as much sense: dams and lodges are intuitive and intelligent constructions invented by beavers to satisfy their needs for comfort, peace and shelter.

Building is rare among mammals. Most have fat paws, hooves or flippers which are useless for construction. And while the clawed paws of armadillos, moles and other burrowers are capable of remarkable excavations, building any sort of nest or shelter with such equipment 'would be like trying to write with a hammer', as two animal biologists put it.[2] Only primates and rodents have dextrous 'hands' capable of the fine movements required for construction. Chimpanzees build sleeping platforms among the branches of trees and harvest mice weave spherical grass nests. But with the exception of human constructions, no mammal-made structure comes close to the complexity of beaver architecture or requires the cognitive acuity to respond to the ever-changing particularities of a riparian environment.

The burned remains of a Haida totem pole.

Onto that singularity of form, add beaver family life. Beavers mate for life; they maintain year-round residence and nurture their offspring well into adolescence. With such startlingly human domestic routines, it is hardly surprising that almost as soon as Europeans made contact with North American beavers, families of building beavers were endlessly anthropomorphized, idealized and romanticized. Beaver architecture was not unknown in Europe, but by the seventeenth century Eurasian beavers were scarce and hard to see. New World adventurers conveniently forgot anything they knew about Old World beavers; dam-building was declared to be a New World marvel, and North American beavers were transfigured into parables of a righteous society. Animals have always been good to think with. Animal societies offer a particular creative freedom within philosophical debate. And a society of animal builders with human-like hands and an uncanny talent for homesteading was a priceless gem.

In the top-left corner of the French cartographer Nicolas de Fer's 1698 map of America is a vignette of Niagara Falls, one of North America's most stunning wonders. Yet the falls are merely a backdrop to an even greater spectacle: no fewer than 52 beavers have joined together to build a dam at the foot of the great Niagara. Some are gnawing at a tree; others carry lumber on their shoulders or mortar on their tails, and one has fallen over, exhausted. Each animal is identified by a letter keyed to a legend, which catalogues the beavers as: (a) lumberjacks who cut big trees with their teeth; (b) carpenters who cut the long branches; (c) bearers of wood for construction; (d) those who make the mortar; (e) commandant or architect; (f) inspector of the disabled; (g) those who drag the mortar on their tails; (h) beaver with a disabled tail from having worked too hard; (i) masons who build the dam; and (l) those who tap with their tails to make the masonry firmer.[3]

Beavers building dams near Niagara Falls, from Nicolas de Fer's map of America (1698).

Beaver falsehoods abound. Beavers do not walk upright carrying logs in their arms; they drag logs with their teeth, and usually through the water. They neither transport mud on their tails nor use their tails as trowels to firm up mud on the dam; beavers carry mud in their arms, sometimes even walking upright, and use their hand-like forepaws to pat the mud firm. It goes without saying that beavers have no commandants or architects, nor are they harassed by 'inspectors of the disabled', who were presumably tasked with weeding out indolent beavers from those with genuine complaints and forcing the lazy beavers to work. And beavers do not gather by the hundreds; a single beaver can build very well, and a single family – consisting of a mating pair and two to four yearlings – is typically the only workforce required.

The beaver vignette was outlandish and charming enough to be copied into London cartographer Herman Moll's 1715 *A New and Exact Map of the Dominions of the King of Great Britain on Ye Continent of North America*, printed in London in 1715. It also appeared in an early eighteenth-century atlas published in Amsterdam, thereby forming part of the romantic imaginary of the three nations most actively engaged in the North American fur trade. In turn, de Fer's image was likely inspired by Nicolas Denys' natural history of North America published in 1672.

A French aristocrat and lieutenant turned explorer, landowner and politician in the New World, Denys first sailed to Acadia in 1632 and lived out his life in New France, founding settlements throughout the Maritime Islands. He wrote extensively on the natural history of his adopted land, but no animal was as singularly impressive to him as the New World beaver. Their tails had the flavour of veal gristle and were very tasty when fried. Their fur was notable, their castoreum goes unmentioned, but what Denys observed 'of the instinct of the Beaver, of their industry, of their discipline, of their subordination, of their obedience in labour, of the greatness of their works' was almost too marvellous to believe: 'I would find it hard to believe myself had I not been an eye-witness thereof.'[4]

According to Denys, 400 beavers gathered to build a dam in early summer. The beavers did not set to work spontaneously, nor did they always labour gladly. An architect was required to decide where and how the dam should be built, and strong-armed foremen ensured a high standard of construction. As de Fer's map illustrated, there were beaver masons, beaver carpenters, ditch diggers, mud movers and log carriers, and each division was supervised by a foreman. Some beavers gnawed down trees while others cut them into stakes and sank them into the river bottom to act as braces for the dam. Other beavers interwove pliant branches between the stakes, and still others brought mud and clay to pack on the dam to solidify its structure and make it watertight. If any beavers were lazy or neglectful of their duty, a foreman 'chastises them, beats them, throws himself on them, and bites them to keep them at their duty'.[5] There was more than a whiff of beaver gulag about Denys's beaver workforce.

Denys claimed that dams stretched 'two hundred paces and more in length'.[6] Subsequent versions of the fable variously doubled or halved that distance, depending on the author's faith in his readers' credulity. But there is a dam in Wood Buffalo National Park in northern Canada that measures 850 m (930 yd), almost fifteen times longer than Denys' 200 paces. To put that into urban perspective, the Wood Buffalo dam is longer than three Manhattan city blocks and 50 m (55 yd) longer than the world's tallest building is tall. Most dams are more modestly sized – between 10 and 200 m (11 and 219 yd) in length – but, likely as not, when Europeans first explored the rivers and forests of North America they encountered phenomenal feats of hydraulic engineering. (Denys suggested that most lakes and ponds in New France had been made by beavers.) Struggling to understand how such extraordinary constructions were possible, Europeans offered an equally extraordinary explanation: hundreds of beavers labouring united.

Denys was the first to publish the fable of North America's beaver collective, but the oldest description of building beavers seems to be Gerald of Wales's account of Welsh beavers from 1188. According to Gerald, the beavers built 'castles' in the river resembling 'a grove of willow trees, rude and natural without, but artfully constructed within'.[7] Gerald did not describe beaver society (and Denys did not mention him), but Gerald did concoct

Herman Moll's engraver copied de Fer's vignette, as the beavers are mirrored in this English map.

his own abrasive theory of beaver cooperation. When tasked with moving particularly large logs, several beavers 'obeying the dictates of nature' lay on their backs while logs were loaded onto their bellies. The beavers and logs were then dragged backwards to the river by other beavers. The Swedish writer Olaus Magnus included an image of a cart beaver in his history of Scandinavia (*History of the Northern Peoples*, 1555), which suggests the trope was reasonably well known across Europe. Yet, oddly or not, although America's beaver workforce is described in every natural history, travelogue and report from the New World until the mid-nineteenth century, cart beavers are mentioned only twice. After four years in the young Massachusetts Bay Colony, William Wood claimed cart duty was beaver slavery rather than instinct or altruism: 'If any

Olaus Magnus included a dam and beaver cart in the middle of his map of Finland, printed in 1555.

131

Beaver accidentally light into a strange place, he is made a drudge so long as he lives there, to carry the greater end of the logge, unless he creepe away by stealth.'[8] The famous French naturalist Georges-Louis Leclerc, Comte de Buffon, dismissed the idea outright.

With the eradication of Eurasian beavers, beaver architecture was lost to the western imagination. But as soon as North American dams and lodges were discovered, building beavers became part of Europe's animal-infused psychology of fables and half-truths used to give meaning and clarity to human experience. The beaver's building prowess suggested beavers were better, smarter and more civilized than other animals, perhaps even humans, and offered moral guidance for human endeavour.

Woman-Beaver also suggested beavers had something significant to offer human society. The Haida myth involves a complex series of withdrawals and returns, with Woman-Beaver ultimately returning, symbolically but potently, to the human world in the crest of Remnants-of-Chewing-Stick. Although the myth revolves around Woman-Beaver's transformation, it is the wandering hunter who returns with a spiritual awakening and a new power garnered from the animal world. But is it the animal world? After all, Woman-Beaver was once a woman. However, the myth was not suggesting that beaver architecture was too remarkable not to have a human foundation, but rather that beaver architecture was too remarkable not to prove the deep connection between the spiritual consciousness of humans and other animals. The natural and supernatural worlds blurred in meaningful ways, and through the crest of Remnants-of-Chewing-Stick, the hunter incorporated the beaver's resourcefulness, craft and ingenuity. Perhaps humans even learned to build from beavers.

Europeans drew very different connections between beaver architecture and human society. If Woman-Beaver required only her two hands and her loneliness to build, European writers maintained that a solitary beaver was far worse than lonely. A single beaver was an embarrassingly mediocre creature. Take Buffon's beaver, for example. As superintendent of the museum and menagerie at the Jardin du Roi in Paris (renamed Muséum National d'Histoire Naturelle after the Revolution), Buffon was at the centre of an expansive network of explorers and naturalists. He was often sent creatures from distant parts of the globe, and in 1758 he was sent a male beaver from Canada.

After a year of acquaintance, Buffon was not impressed. The beaver was peaceable but prone to melancholy and other gloomy moods. He seemed indifferent to most things, formed no attachments and was scarcely able to defend himself. Worse, he was a jumble of parts, with the backend of a fish and the front half of a rodent. In Buffon's opinion, the lumbersome beaver would be one gross anatomical mistake if it were not for the astonishing attribute of beaver conviviality. For Buffon, beaver dams were 'the fruits of a perfected society' and beavers were the perfect citizens: 'Having moderate appetites, and an aversion to flesh and blood, they have not the smallest propensity to hostilities or rapine, but actually enjoy all those blessings which man knows only how to desire.' Although Buffon had no acquaintance with the animals in the wild, and although he had only met one gloomy, captive beaver, for him, beavers offered the hope of utopia. It was an extraordinary leap of the imagination. Yet it was a leap Enlightenment thinkers were more than willing to take.

In a sense, a single beaver like Buffon's offers an animal counterpoint to the lonely wild men of the woods and feral children that so delighted European philosophers. Just as beavers could only build as part of a collective, they would only build in the wilderness: 'They never attempt to build in countries where they are in danger of having their tranquillity interrupted.'[9] Dislocated from

A beaver mask carved from alder wood made by the Tlingit nation of the Pacific Northwest coast, *c.* 1870.

his beaver society and trapped in a human world, Buffon's beaver had lost his community, his language and his purpose.

Of course these were the questions of the Enlightenment. How did societies become civilized? What was humanity's place within the natural world? And was society a corrupting force or was political structure the only thing saving humans from chaos? Within Buffon's philosophical musings, society was not simply a gathering of individuals. What made beavers praiseworthy was their desire to work peaceably for their mutual benefit without greed, hierarchy or violence. The question for Buffon was how beavers, and by extension humans, might achieve their greatest, happiest and fullest potential.

134

Bob Verschueren's sculpture of branches and logs echoes the organic form and growth of beaver architecture: *Installation xv/13 'La Coulée'*, Conservatoire et Jardin Botanique de la Ville de Genève, 2003, wood.

Writing nearly a century before and a world away, Denys framed his beaver gulag according to a very different set of principles. Luxuriating in the fantasy of hundreds of well-disciplined workers labouring to erect large public works, Denys was perhaps thinking of his fellow colonialists in New France. In 1632 when he arrived in Acadia, the settlement was a few dozen years old and populated primarily by itinerant fur traders. Life was dangerous and unsteady in the New World. (After its fur licence was revoked in 1607, Acadia was re-established in 1610 but required rebuilding in 1613 after British forces burned it to the ground.) The land was heavily forested and needed clearing to farm; the settlers were small in number and likely daunted by

A beaver village was built by dedicated teamwork and cooperative effort.

the difficulty of life. Throughout New France land tenure was essentially feudal. Large parcels known as 'seigneuries' were granted to nobles, military officers and clergy, who rented smaller plots to tenants, known as habitants. The habitants cleared the land, built their homes and paid rent in wheat and livestock, but it was the seigneurs who took on the investment of building a mill or road. By 1671, the first census of Acadia counted 392 people, less than Denys's 400-strong beaver labour force, and less than the colony's 484 cows and 524 sheep. Even in the wilds of North America, even if it meant whipping grunt labour into action, a society based on civil obedience, subordination and hard labour could achieve magnificent, awe-inspiring works with a beaver chain gang as a moral guide.

Most versions of beaver society were remarkably strict. In his account of New France from 1708, a surgeon-explorer known only by the surname Dièreville claimed beavers had no need of foremen since all beavers were vigilant disciplinarians. At the least sign of laziness, indolent workers were immediately beaten by their neighbours and brought to heel, or cast out of society: 'Justice is everything among beavers.'[10] In 1827, the French Romantic François-René de Chateaubriand (for whom the steak was named) claimed that if any beaver 'citizen' refused his share of public burdens, he was banished, his fur was stripped from his back as a mark of infamy, and he was forced to live in a hole by himself in disgrace.[11] These vagabond beavers were called terriers, from the French word for earth, *terre*. Their fur was inferior, dirty, scrubby and useless to the fur trade – a double damnation.

Building beavers were never just beavers who built, and beaver societies offered correctives to a variety of social vices. Outcast beavers could be read as moral lessons for young men tempted to abandon the sparse civility of colonial life for the fur trade. Independent and unregulated as they sought their fortunes in fur, *coureurs de bois* – or runners of the woods, as traders were known – lived closely with indigenous communities, married aboriginal women and were naturally vilified by the bourgeois fur merchants and ruling classes. Some writers saw beavers as countering vices perceived in aboriginal communities. The character of the 'Ignoble Indian' crafted by Europeans was indolent and itinerant, whereas beavers were industrious, intolerant of sloth and built sturdy, permanent homes.[12] The Jesuit priest Pierre François-Xavier de Charlevoix, for example, scorned Iroquoian villages as 'a confused heap of cabbins . . . built with much less art, neatness, and solidity than those of the beavers'.[13] In sharp contrast, the idealist Louis-Armand de Lom d'Arce, Baron de Lahontan, saw beavers as mirroring everything to be admired in the aboriginal way of life.

Lahontan is a fascinating character in the ideological construction of the New World. With the early death of his father, he came to his title in 1674 at the young age of eight, joined the military at seventeen and arrived in the New World in 1683. He spent a decade in New France, exploring the region and learning the languages and cultures of neighbouring first Nations. Although he was promoted to king's lieutenant in 1692, he deserted the army shortly after. Unable to return to France, and having lost his inheritance, Lahontan went to Amsterdam where he published his works including his final and most famous, *Supplement aux voyages ou dialogues avec le sauvage Adario*, which criticized all the political corruption, religious persecution and social inequality he had witnessed in France.

Based around an imaginary dialogue between Lahontan and a Huron chief named Adario, *Supplement aux voyages* sharply contrasted Old World tyrannies with the freedoms and justice of North America's Aboriginal Nations. His idealized view of humans living in a pure and natural state offered an early expression of the potent Enlightenment trope of the 'Noble Savage', and although Lahontan never makes the link explicit, there is much to compare between Lahontan's visions of Aboriginal Nations and beaver societies. Lahontan's beavers lived a good, happy, gentle and above all egalitarian existence, with peace and harmony as their primary goals. According to local people (perhaps the Meskwaki), beavers had a language of 'bemoaning inarticulate Sounds' by which they communally agreed on what needed to be done to maintain their lodges, dams, lakes and the peaceable order of their republic. In Lahontan's eyes, beavers and first Nations shared equally in the blissful freedom of the Americas while escaping all the oppression and injustice plaguing the Old World.

But why do beavers build? Evolutionary biologists have shown that deep water is central to a beaver's survival. Dam building is the animal's industrious solution to ensure lakes are always deep enough to escape predators and keep the lodge entrance submerged. Lodges are warmer than burrows and, in the centre of a deep lake, are untouchable by most predators.

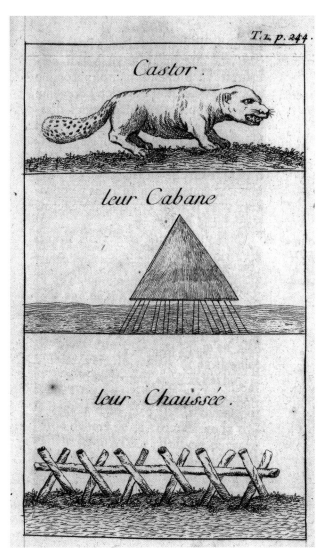

Castor.

leur Cabane

leur Chaussée.

T. 1. p. 244.

Early descriptions claimed beavers built their lodges on stilts. Antoine-Simon Le Page du Pratz, *History of Louisiana* (1758).

Although Eurasian beavers are somewhat less inclined to build than North American beavers, both species can live in either burrows or lodges, depending on the environmental situation. Dams are not absolutely necessary to the beaver's way of life; they are only required to regulate and raise the flow of water. Where rivers are deep and fast flowing and banks are high, beavers often forgo building altogether. Lodge-building beavers also frequently dig themselves one or several burrows as a precautionary measure. Yet, for centuries naturalists maintained that Old World beavers had long since abandoned their architectural arts.

Buffon spent some time considering why Eurasian beavers had ceased building. His answer was simple: humans had broken their will. In fact, humans had oppressed the animals throughout Europe.

Beavers often build multiple lodges on a pond.

> As man becomes civilized and improved, other animals
> are repressed and degraded. Reduced to servitude, or treated
> as rebels, and dispersed by force, all their societies are dis-
> solved, and their talents rendered nugatory; their arts have
> disappeared, and they now retain nothing but their solitary
> instincts.

As Buffon looked around at the few beavers remaining in France, he saw solitary, timid and forlorn terriers. They never gathered into societies and so could never erect great works. 'The only remaining monument of that ancient intelligence in brutes' to be found anywhere in the world was the North American beaver.[14] Such praise was particularly notable as Buffon considered the New World and all its organic productions to be inherently defective.

The ancient theory of geographical determinism held that the climate and location of a place – its altitude, proximity to open water, temperature, humidity, prevalence of winds, and so on – fundamentally shaped the character of its flora and fauna. Since nature was a harmonious whole, the overarching environmental conditions offered a sort of intricate geographical map from which the annual rainfall could be read as easily as the size of cows and the quantity of venomous snakes. The philosophy was malleable, and easily shaped to prove any nation's superiority or damn it to mediocrity, but generally speaking a pleasantly warm and dry climate was considered most auspicious. Buffon described North America as a cold and dank sponge.

Since the New World forests had not been cut, Buffon argued, the nourishing heat of the sun never warmed the soil or evaporated the standing water. In this gloomy, unwholesome atmosphere, organic nature languished. New World animals were smaller, less vigorous and less diverse than Old World species, except insects and reptiles, which thrived in bogs. European sheep wasted under

A large beaver
dam.

the watery American sun; their flesh became less juicy and tough.
Humans were also affected. A cold and languid people, Buffon's
aboriginals were small and hairless with shrunken penises. They
had neither ardour for their women nor the temper for society.
And although more nimble than Europeans, 'being habituated
to running', they were weak, timid and dastardly, with no vivacity
of mind or body.[15] But beavers, despite being architects of Buffon's
dreaded marshes, transcended every limiting condition of their
climate.

Buffon conceded that once its bogs were drained, America
would become 'most fruitful, healthy, and opulent'. He even noted
several species beside the beaver which had 'improved their original nature by the influence of the soil and climate'.[16] But such
small praise did little to soften his broad damnation. Some authors
took his argument further and claimed European colonists also

degenerated in the New World, damned their descendants to ever more dull-witted and withered lives.

Naturally Buffon's theories did not sit well in America. In fact, Thomas Jefferson dedicated the largest section of his *Notes on the State of Virginia* to debunking Buffon. Published in 1785, just two years after Jefferson wrote the Declaration of Independence, *Notes on the State* laboriously detailed the achievement of Americans (both indigenous and imported), exalted America's natural resources and included extensive tables comparing the various sizes of North American and European animals. According to Jefferson, American bears weighed 185 kg (410 lb); imported cows swelled to 1,100 kg (2,500 lb), and North American beavers weighed 20 kg (45 lb). In

A woman examines the stump of a tree felled by beavers, Bow River, Alberta, 1954.

contrast European animals were measly little beasts. Bears weighed just 70 kg (155 lb, the size of a sheep), cows a mere 345 kg (760 lb, a little more than a just-weaned calf) and beavers snuck in at 8 kg (18½ lb, the size of a large dachshund). The absurdity of shrinking European species down to sheep, calves and toy dogs hints at an underlying anxiety; there was more at stake than simply defending the new republic's domestic productions.

The American War of Independence ended in 1783 with a peace treaty that marked the thirteen states' separation from British rule. Despite its successes, the young republic was unsteady and troubled by conflict. Moreover, early American political theorists argued that the originary seed of American republicanism lay between its people and their soil: by clearing the wilderness and building their homes, early settlers had cultivated their rights and freedoms. In a sense, nature had produced a distinctly republican state. If that nature was inherently degenerate, the republic's collapse would be inevitable.[17]

Beavers were an obvious symbol for the young republic. They had long been the backbone of the American economy and had already assisted in clearing the forests. Even the venerable Buffon agreed New World beavers were vastly superior, larger and had better fur than European stock. Most importantly, by simply living their lives and doing what came naturally, beavers embodied the republic's values of industry, prudence and civic responsibility. Beavers were never surprised by the suddenness or severity of winters, but had the foresight to store food during the summer months. They diligently extracted every goodness nature had to give, which dovetailed with the political belief that industrious homesteaders would guarantee the health, happiness and survival of the nation's republican institutions. As the historian Peter Messer explains: 'The foundations of the republic had literally been laid by the industrious work of the beaver. All that Americans had to

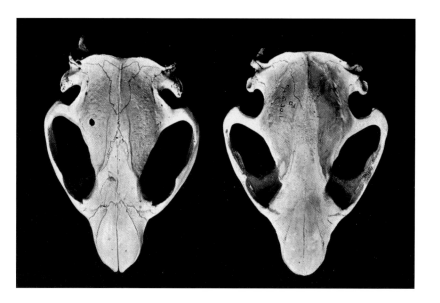

do was embrace the same penchant for improvement.'[18] And, in a sense, all republican naturalists had to do was turn Buffon's words against him. For American political theorists, Old World oppression begat timorous beasts, whether human, beaver or otherwise.

A Eurasian beaver skull on the left and a North American skull on the right.

Although not as long-lived as the fable of the beaver's musky testicles, the society of the building beaver had all the right endowments to make it equally beloved. Beaver dams and lodges were genuinely extraordinary, and could only be seen in North America. Moreover, Aristotle and Pliny never mentioned beaver architecture. That the phenomenon was perceived to be a previously unknown animal talent and an attribute of a newly discovered continent, added an allegorical intensity to the myth and made it particularly appealing to writers who were wrestling with new ways of understanding human society. North America's building beavers stepped outside age-old debates and offered fresh intellectual meat, so to speak. And perhaps that enjoyment of novelty explains why beaver societies populate the literature of colonists, founders of new republics and Enlightenment visionaries. The ever-extraordinary beaver offered extraordinary hope for a better future.

But of course, flaunting the beaver as an exemplary citizen had a dark underbelly. At the very same moment that philosophical beavers sparkled, skinned carcasses were piling up to keep haberdasheries in good supply. Surprising or not, writers discussed beavers as both commodities and cultured citizens, almost within the same breath. In a manner not altogether different from John Berger's famous observation of the peasant who is fond of his pig *and* glad to salt away his pork, Charlevoix writes:

> the spoil of this animal has hitherto been the principal article in the commerce of New France. It is itself one of the greatest wonders in nature, and may very well afford many a striking lesson of industry, foresight, dexterity, and perseverance in labour.[19]

Charlevoix's words remind us that, for all the praise, the building beaver collective was just an allegory for human musings. Although writers truly believed beavers gathered by the hundreds to build a communal dam, the resonance of the idea was far more important than its truth. Animal fables have never been lessons in animal rights.

The duplicity of slaughtering the embodiment of animal civility was not lost on all writers. A son of the French Revolution, Chateaubriand politicized the beaver betrayal, suggesting that 'man allows the ferocious beasts to live and exterminates the beavers, as he endured tyrants and persecutes innocence and genius'.[20] But more often than not the beaver's demise was simply accepted as the inevitable way of progress. As Buffon suggested, human development squelched animal genius. At best animals were reduced to slavery; at worse they were exterminated. While the loss was surely lamentable, it hardly outweighed the moral imperative for human advancement. 'It is a subject of regret that an animal so valuable and prolific should be hunted in a manner tending so evidently to the extermination of the species', John Godman wrote in 1831 in his *American Natural History*. 'The race will eventually be extinguished', he stated with a morbid confidence. 'A few individuals may, for a time, elude the immediate violence of persecution and . . . be occasionally exhibited as melancholy mementos of tribes long previously whelmed in the fathomless gulf of avarice.'[21]

If societies of building beavers jarred against the reality of the fur trade, they also came up against various scientific notions of animal intelligence. By suggesting that beavers communicated and reasoned among themselves, writers attributed to them a high degree of understanding. Most controversial was beaver language. No matter how bemoaning or authoritarian the tones, beavers expressed their wishes, collaborated and ordered each other about. Such beaver communication challenged the philosophies of René Descartes, who famously argued that animals were nothing more than clockwork creatures. For Descartes, language and the capacity to communicate meaning were the principle signs of human intelligence. Animals' lack of language signalled their corresponding lack of conscious intent.

A century later, and for very different reasons, Frédéric Cuvier denied beavers any glimmer of intelligence. Head keeper of the menagerie at the Muséum National d'Histoire Naturelle from 1804 to 1838 and younger brother of the great anatomist George, Cuvier was well acquainted with the lives and ways of animals, at least in captivity, and had no problem ascribing a high degree of understanding to a female orang-utan. But beavers were rodents, and rodents were lowly. Cuvier argued that animal intelligence gradually increased from rodents to ruminants, through pachyderms and carnivores, finally ascending to the superior heights of a primate's brain. Building beavers challenged Cuvier's tidy assessment, but the solution was easy: he simply ascribed their talents to instinct. Observing several beavers that had been taken from their parents at a young age, Cuvier noted that even without parental guidance these beavers built, urged on by the blind, mechanical force of instinct. Whereas intelligent acts arose from experience and instruction, instinct was an innate and irresistible force.

Beaver advocates attacked such philosophical hierarchies on all sides. In his second collection of fables from 1678, Jean de La

The compulsive work ethic of beaver.

148

BEAVER HUNTING in CANADA.

Fontaine argued against Descartes' clockwork creatures with specific instances of animal ingenuity. La Fontaine pointed to the cleverness of a mother partridge who pretends to have a broken wing to draw the hunter from her young, to the stratagems of a pursued stag, and to the extraordinary communal building practices of North American beavers: 'To such a colony of cunning amphibians the republic of Plato itself would be but an apprentice affair.' The animals simply evidenced too much skill, community and industry to be purely driven by mechanical instinct: 'That these beavers are nothing but bodies without minds nothing will make me believe.'[22]

Likewise, in his work on animal intelligence the French zoologist Ernest Menault argued against Cuvier by claiming instinct and intelligence were not mutually exclusive: instinctual urges could be shaped and improved by intelligence and training. Menault also observed the building habits of captive beavers, but to very different effect. One night, snow was blowing into a beaver's cage. The animal had only a few branches, some litter, carrots and apples. By morning it had interlaced the branches between the bars of its cage, 'just as a basket-maker would have done', and filled the gaps with the litter and food.[23] Instinct urged the beaver to build, but intelligence enabled the animal to adapt to circumstances.

It was precisely such ingenious architectural responses to environmental particularities that confirmed beaver intelligence for Lewis Henry Morgan. An American lawyer and statesman, but best known for his anthropological work, Morgan was something of a nineteenth-century polymath. He was also a director and shareholder in a railway company, and it was on a stretch of railway connecting Detroit to an iron ore discovery on the southern shore of Lake Superior that Morgan became impassioned with beavers. For more than a decade, he dedicated himself to

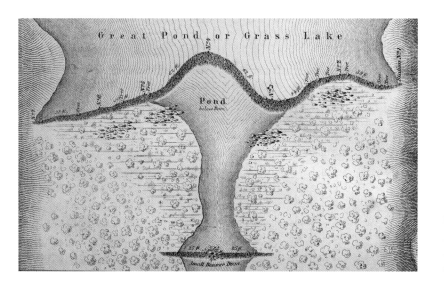

Great Pond or Grass Lake

Pond
below Dam.

Small Beaver Dam

scrutinizing every inch of the animal's anatomy and lifestyle. The result was *The America Beaver and His Works*, published in 1868, the first comprehensive study of beaver architecture.

It so happened that the railway passed through a pristine wilderness inhabited by a thriving community of beavers. From the size of the dams and beaver meadows, Morgan judged the animals had been at work for centuries, apparently undisturbed by the fur trade. As he measured the height and length of each dam, broke open abandoned lodges, dug out burrows and admired the extent of artificial lakes, the facts of beaver construction became more marvellous to him than the fantasy of a hundred-strong beaver workforce.

In an area of 13 by 10 km (8 by 6 miles), Morgan counted no fewer than 63 beaver dams, ranging from 15 to 150 m (50 to 500 ft) in length. He estimated one dam to contain approximately 450,000 kg (100,000 lb) of material. Another was 3.5 m (12 ft) tall.

Sophisticated hydroengineering is required to maintain the solidity of large beaver dams.

151

With so many dams to examine, Morgan was able to determine that, although they were all constructed according to the same basic principles, each dam was uniquely and ingeniously adapted to its ever-changing environment. He observed that larger dams were curved at the centre, a hydroengineering trick which distributed the water's pressure and protected the dam from being overwhelmed. Dams also had outlets to drain off surplus water that threatened to damage dam or flood lodges. Morgan was equally impressed by lodge design, particularly after he climbed inside a lodge to take a peek. And with his dedicated fieldwork, Morgan was the first to describe beaver canals. These extraordinary excavations were, in Morgan's opinion, 'the highest act of intelligence and knowledge performed by beavers'.[24]

Once beavers have taken down the trees closest to their pond, they must seek trees further from the water's safety. Moreover, their preferred hardwoods rarely grow in swampy soil, and trees often die when beavers flood an area. But foraging far from water is difficult and dangerous work. Even if a beaver did trudge overland towards a stand of aspen, and did succeed in chewing down a tree over several hours without being heard by a predator, the animal would then have to haul the log back to its pond. Where ground is uneven or covered in dense underbrush, dragging the log would be all but impossible. And if the noise attracted unwelcome attention, the beaver would be stranded without water for escape. To avoid all such problems, beavers excavate a network of canals to provide watery safety while foraging and a means of floating logs home. Morgan observed shortcuts dug through bends in meandering streams and dams built across canals to help store extra water. He even found a canal that branched into two when it reached a hardwood forest on a hill, giving the beavers 65 m (215 ft) of forest frontage. Like Menault, Morgan concluded that instinct might urge beavers to dig a canal towards the forest, but

Beaver canal, measuring 80 m (265 ft) along its longest arm.

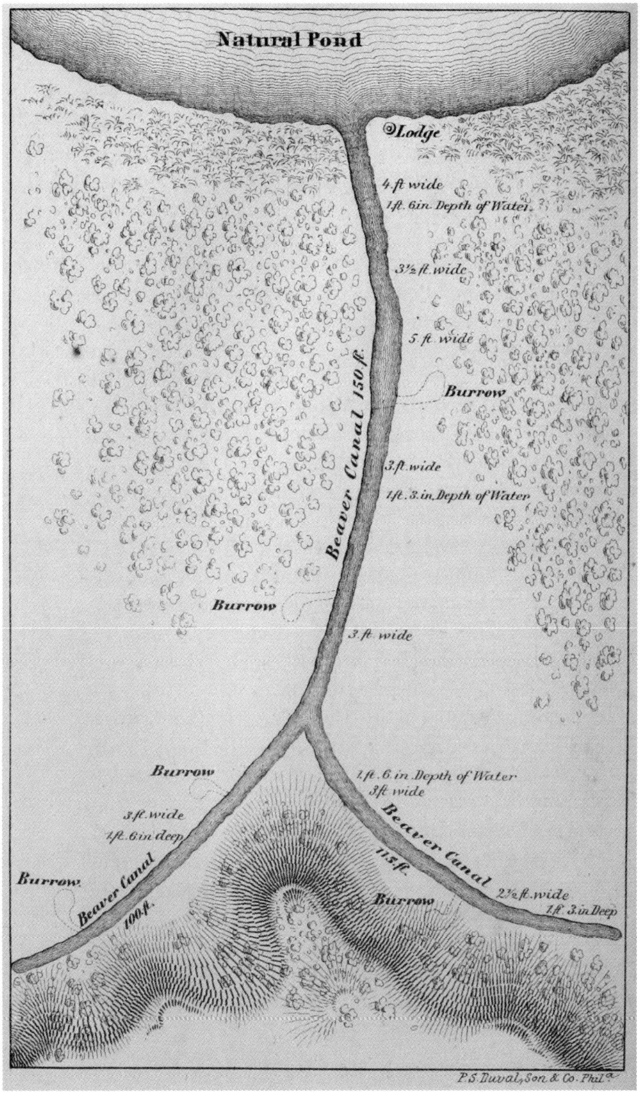

Natural Pond

Lodge

4 ft wide
1 ft. 6 in. Depth of Water

3½ ft. wide

5 ft wide

Burrow

3 ft. wide

1 ft. 3 in. Depth of Water

Beaver Canal 150 ft.

Burrow

3 ft. wide

Burrow

1 ft. 6 in. Depth of Water
3 ft. wide

Beaver Canal

3 ft. wide
1 ft. 6 in. deep

115 ft.

Burrow

Beaver Canal

100 ft.

Burrow

2½ ft. wide
1 ft. 3 in. Deep

P. S. Duval, Son. & Co. Philᵃ

only a keen understanding of the environment's advantages could motivate such resourcefulness.

For Morgan, building was the physical manifestation of beaver intelligence, and the animals seemed inspired by the sheer pleasures of construction. 'When a beaver stands for a moment and looks upon his work, evidently to see whether it is right, and whether anything else is needed, he shows himself capable of . . . his own mental processes.'[25] And in that, Morgan suggests something akin to the Haida myth of Woman-Beaver, who built to enhance her enjoyment of life and the landscape, compelled by a natural urge and guided by her creative intelligence. Even for the casual observer, dams will always seem too remarkably and idiosyncratically designed for its particular environmental situation to be simply the product of an instinctual drive. Lodges can be 12 m (40 ft) across, 3 m (10 ft) high and have more than 3,000 kg (6,500 lb) of logs and mud. When encountered by chance, deep within the wilderness and surrounded by silence, such works

The mystic beauty of a beaver lodge in mid-winter.

are awe-inspiring, even mystically beautiful, and offer compelling evidence that intelligent forces are at work in the forest.

Perhaps because beavers are nocturnal and semiaquatic, only a few research projects have examined beaver intelligence. In one study, two beavers were confined to an enclosure with a pool and a few decorative trees for shade. The researchers tried to save the trees by wrapping them with wire mesh. One night the beavers used branches to build ramps up the trees so they could gnaw them down above the wire. Intrigued, the researchers put pieces of bread on the top of metre-high poles. Again the beavers built foraging ramps, but only to the poles with bread. Beavers have also been tested with puzzle boxes, and seem to be one of the few animals with the optimal combination of brains, manual (or beak) dexterity and perseverance to work through the series of locks and fasteners to get to the food inside.

But such artificial testing seems whimsical compared to beavers' responses to real-life contingencies. In a sense, beaver architecture itself offers insight into a beaver's brain. Invisible cognitive processes are physically worked out with sticks, mud and water as beavers fix leaks, dig shortcuts through meandering streams or cobble together unorthodox materials to repair badly broken dams as quickly as possible. Beavers are obviously driven by instinct to build, but their craft is honed over a lifetime of work. James and Carol Gould have suggested that dam construction reflects learned cultural variation between beaver districts. 'Almost everything about the actions of these rodents suggests that they employ concepts and reasoning to power their behaviour', the Goulds write in their study of animal architecture. Having solved the major problems of food and predation, beavers have the free time to dream, as it were: 'Imagination, an ability to plan, and a ready willingness to learn from experience seem the most realistic combination of cognitive faculties' driving the building beaver.[26]

While most beaver lovers have tried to save beaver architecture from the damnation of instinct, Bernard Rudofsky, an Austrian-American architect, designer and outspoken critic of modern design, lauded beaver instinct as a human salvation. Best remembered for his 1964 MOMA exhibit 'Architecture without Architects', Rudofsky saw a purity of architectural design in the anonymous architecture of huts, caves, ancient sepulchres, beehives and beaver dams. Growing from physical needs and dimensions, without frills or fashions, such dwellings were external expressions of being: 'Habit has begotten habitation.' Rudofsky most admired the innate building know-how of animals. 'Since natural instincts are lost under domestication', a line Rudofsky lifted from *On the Origin of Species*, 'man, that most overdomesticated mammal, has nothing to fall back on.' In contrast to the excesses and egos of modern architecture, animals build intuitively and beautifully to their needs.

Sunrise on a beaver pond.

Maura Doyle, *Get the Bread*, 2009, bread, metal pole, wood, unfired clay, sticks. An interpretation of a beaver intelligence test.

Writing in the late 1960s and '70s, with a growing fatigue for modern architecture, Rudofsky upheld the perfect instinctual simplicity of beaver building as an aesthetic, almost spiritual tonic. 'We had better be informed about the finer points of animal architecture and engineering', Rudofsky urged, 'in order to preserve our humaneness. On the whole we can learn from animals a good deal more than they can learn from us.'[27] A society of building beavers might yet teach us how to live.

5 Ecologist

The animal supreme of all the forest, they were the
Wilderness personified, the Wild articulate, the Wild
that was our home.
Grey Owl, *Pilgrims of the Wild* (1935)

The busy lives of beavers were first captured on film in a thirteen-
minute silent movie shot in 1928. *The Beaver People*, directed by
Bill Oliver and produced by the Dominion Parks Branch and
the National Film Board of Canada, centred on the pioneering
environmental work of Grey Owl, Canada's voice of the wilderness
in the 1930s. Continuing in the tradition of Henry David Thoreau
and Ralph Waldo Emerson, Grey Owl warned against the threat
civilization brought to Canada's remaining wild places. As the
landscape was settled, its resources exploited and its wildlife
hunted into extinction, Grey Owl urged a more vivid awareness
and respect for the Canadian wilderness and respite for all its
creaturely life, but most especially for its most iconic animal, 'the
animal supreme of all the forest', the beaver.

In the early twentieth century, the secretive ways of the beaver
were little known and rarely observed except by trappers and
dedicated woodsmen. In their cinematic debut they proved
themselves wildly charismatic. From their home deep within the
Canadian woods, the beavers charmed viewers as they waddled
and splashed, ate apples offered to them, groomed their plump
bellies and wrestled with Grey Owl's wife Anahareo. They were
more like pets than wild animals, which made the fur trade all
the more appalling. As one of the film's intertitles read, 'Ruthless
greed and slaughter have reduced his magnificent race, once

Grey Owl shares his canoe with a beaver.

numbering ten million, to a mere remnant and awakened the sympathy of even his former enemies.' Canada had long defined itself as a land of inexhaustible resources, and beavers had taken the brunt of this self-serving fantasy.

Grey Owl had undergone his own sympathetic awakening, having made his living by trapping until the day Anahareo found two orphaned beaver kits. Their mother had been killed by one of Grey Owl's traps. At Anahareo's insistence, the couple raised the kits, fed them milk and porridge and named them McGinnis and McGinty, perhaps as a nod to Grey Owl's supposed half-Scot, half-Apache heritage. The beavers offered 'almost childlike intimacies and murmurings of affection', Grey Owl later wrote.

'They seemed to be almost like little folk from some other planet, whose language we could not yet quite understand. To kill such creatures seemed monstrous.'[1] From that day, Grey Owl left off trapping for ever and turned to writing and activism to support his family.

Grey Owl feeding a baby beaver.

He was wildly successful. In his books, films and lecture tours across North America and Britain, including performances at Harvard University and Buckingham Palace, Grey Owl wrote and spoke movingly about the vanishing wilderness and the plight of its creatures. The Dominion Parks Branch (now Parks Canada) recruited Grey Owl in 1931 to work as a naturalist and caretaker in Manitoba's Riding Mountain National Park and, later, in Prince Albert National Park in Saskatchewan, with the aim of establishing a beaver sanctuary. Dressed in buckskins, moccasins, braids and feathers, Grey Owl preached a nostalgic and poetic message of shedding the yoke of civilization and returning to simpler times. When met with the soulful appreciation and sense of wonder that Grey Owl accredited to his aboriginal heritage, nature was a spiritual cleanser from the ills of modern life.

But Grey Owl was not what he appeared to be. After his death, his English heritage was exposed. Grey Owl was born Archibald Stansfeld Belaney in the town of Hastings in East Sussex and had arrived in Canada as a young man in 1906. Over his years in the Canadian backcountry, Belaney reinvented himself, dyed his hair black, adopted the traditional dress and lifestyle of the Ojibwe and became fluent in their language. Belaney became Grey Owl before he converted to wildlife preservation, but his adopted culture added an emotional intensity to his message. As an aboriginal, Grey Owl embodied the romantic image of a disappearing wilderness, its people and a way of life for a mostly white viewing audience.

Grey Owl's beavers were not entirely what they seemed either. The beavers were not portrayed as wild animals so much as points of nationalized nostalgia. Cute and chubby with a Disneyesque charm, they were reimagined as childlike victims of thoughtless exploitation. As Canada's imperilled little brothers, the beavers symbolized a threatened, defanged and declawed nature, not the ruthless wilderness of a pack of wolves bringing a moose, but a vulnerable and evocative wildness that reminded viewers of how much they had to lose.

But that is only one way to see a beaver. The previous chapters explore how beavers have been fragmented and manhandled, both metaphorically and literally, into parables and materials for human self-representation. For millennia, beavers were absent, too few in number and too symbolically compelling to be seen as living creatures. But beavers are back, and with extraordinary vigour. It may still be hard to see the nocturnal and aquatic animals, but evidence of their activity is increasingly hard to miss.

Our last beaver romance draws the animals out from the half-light and into the spotlight. The ecological beaver makes international news and sparks impassioned environmental debates across the globe from California to Mongolia to Tierra del Fuego. What makes the ecological beaver different from the musky, fur or architectural beavers, is its vital connection with the landscape. Like the canary in the mine shaft, the ecological beaver is synonymous with the health of woodlands, wetlands and riparian habitats.

However, seeing a beaver is always a matter of perspective, and the ecological beaver is hardly the exception. By simply living

Beavers take over residence of an abandoned farm.

their lives and doing what comes naturally, beavers are heralded as climate change heroes by some and as agents of ecological devastation by others. As ever, to interpret a culture's beaver is to read their book of nature. But before we can gauge the benefits of beaver ecology, the animals have to be brought back to life.

For centuries, trappers and naturalists on both continents lamented dwindling beaver populations without expending much effort to stop the eradication. Norway passed Europe's earliest beaver protection law in 1845, an act which likely saved the Scandinavian beaver population, but most countries were hardly so enlightened. Sweden banned beaver hunting in 1873, two years after Swedish beavers were already extinct. By the end of the nineteenth century, eight isolated populations totalling a mere 1,200 animals were all that remained of the Eurasian beaver.

North American beavers fared only slightly better. By the 1800s, beavers were critically threatened from coast to coast, even in the vast expanse of the Canadian north. The population may have dipped as low as 100,000 animals, and it is partly due to the early conservation efforts of George Simpson, governor of Hudson's Bay Company for the better part of four decades, that North American beavers survived the nineteenth century. When George Simpson was appointed head of the company's Northern Department in 1821 he was saddled with rehabilitating a desperately overhunted territory. In 1824, he travelled by canoe from Hudson's Bay westward to the Pacific Ocean to see the landscape for himself. He was horrified. After almost a month on the waterways that had once been the lifeblood of the fur trade, Simpson never saw a beaver. 'We did not see a single animal . . . exceeding the size of a Musk Rat and not so much as the vestige of a Beaver.'[2] Drastic and unpopular measures were required. Although he banned beaver hunting throughout the region, Simpson had no

direct power to stop trappers. Instead, he implemented various conservation policies. He prohibited the distribution of any more steel traps, offered higher rates for other pelts (particularly muskrat) and closed trading posts in trapped-out areas, while opening posts in areas with comparatively stable beaver populations.

Simpson was not always so conservationally minded. In 1827, in the hopes of deterring America's westward expansion, he initiated a beaver eradication programme through the Oregon Territory, an area that stretched along the Pacific coast from the northern part of present-day California to southern Alaska. Since 'the first step that the American Government will take towards Colonization is through their Indian Traders', Simpson argued, 'if the country becomes exhausted in Fur bearing animals they can have no

An albino beaver in the Biologiska Museet in Stockholm.

The Hudson's Bay Company's conservation initiatives continued into the 20th century; here, live beavers are transferred to Charlton Island Preserve, 1939.

inducement to proceed thither'. He gave instructions to wipe out every beaver and other furry creature that might be valuable to the Americans. 'The country is a rich preserve of Beaver and which for political reasons we should endeavour to destroy as soon as possible.'[3]

And yet, within lands safely under the governance of the Hudson's Bay Company, Simpson viewed beaver as a precious commodity that had been severely damaged by thoughtless exploitation. With the company's fortunes at stake, Simpson transformed the beaver trade of the Canadian North into a sustainable resource. He even helped established the world's first beaver sanctuary on Charlton Island at the southern tip of Hudson's Bay. The island was purged of predators, trapping was forbidden, and in 1836, 28 beavers were released. Within a decade, at least 60 lodges were spotted. By 1851, beavers were so numerous on the island that Simpson ordered 5,000 to be trapped.[4]

The numbers seem astonishing, but if all offspring of the original fourteen pairs survived, in ten years Charlton Island could have had as many as 10,000 beavers. After a decade, mortality rates set in (beavers usually live for about eight to twelve years, although twenty-year-old beavers are not uncommon). Food supply might become limited and beaver-congested watersheds could affect population growth, preventing young beavers from establishing their own home range. But in an optimal, predator-free habit with abundant food and water, the population on Charlton Island could easily have exceeded 25,000 beavers in the fifteen years between 1836 and 1851.

The extraordinary recovery rests squarely on beavers' evolutionary superiority. As long as beavers have trees and water, they can remodel most landscapes to suit their tastes. If the water is too shallow for safety, beavers build a dam. If the trees grow sparse, they dig a canal to access better food and lumber. Beavers have even been known to use stones and greenery in their dams, if

Boys and 2-week-old beaver kits at the Rupert's House beaver preserve, c. 1942.

required. The same survival skills that enabled them to withstand millions of years of environmental change, ice ages, droughts and predation ensured that beavers would thrive just as soon as their most successful predator, humans, the only one beavers did not evolve to resist, converted to conservation.

The early twentieth century is marked by new ways of knowing and appreciating nature – particularly the new science of ecology and rising concerns for species loss and environmental degradation. Although ecology would not become a significant intellectual force in environmental management until the mid-twentieth century, knowing how beavers lived within their environments was crucial to most beaver conservation initiatives. Beavers were not simply deposited into landscapes and forgotten: they were monitored, their kits and lodges were counted, and their lifestyles and dietary preferences observed and documented.

Dolly Jørgensen, an environmental historian of Nordic fauna, offers a remarkable account of Sweden's early beaver reintroduction programmes. Sweden lost its last native beaver in the 1870s. Half a century later, between 1922 and 1940, 80 Norwegian beavers were introduced in the hopes of repopulating the landscape. The second programme, organized in 1924 by a Swedish wildlife and hunting association, released seven Norwegian beavers into northern Sweden. The act itself was not unique, but the language recorded in the official documentation is remarkable.

The release was overseen by a 'baptismal officiant' and attended by 'godparents' who were sponsoring each set of beavers. 'The use of these titles', Jørgensen observes, 'signals that the people present at the reintroduction were more than observers – they became the people responsible for the beaver's future success.' As with Christian baptisms, in which godparents guide a child's initiation

Beaver introduction at Harrsjön, Görviksjön, in 1925.

and growth within the Christian community, the beavers' sponsors agreed to help the animals find their place and thrive within the Swedish national landscape. And like Christian sponsorship, the relationship was steadfast and enduring. The godparents not only consented to continuing financial support, but maintained a heartfelt, perhaps even spiritual, connection to the newly baptized Swedish beavers. Members of the association reported where beaver tracks and lodges could be seen and when young beavers were spotted. Although many of the godparents were hunters, beaver hunting was never mentioned in the association's articles. 'Instead, these hunters felt they had to nurture nature as a godfather, to watch over the beavers and help them succeed in their new homes because previous hunters had failed to take care of them.'[5] A precious piece of Nordic fauna was returning, and its rite of initiation was a step towards rehabilitating the Swedish landscape itself.

Other animals, such as muskox, were also reintroduced and also symbolized the returning fitness of the natural and national landscape. But few animals could justify the ideologically laden rhetoric of baptism with as little irony as beavers. Beavers offer a human likeness; their domestic routines and industrious ways suggest they are something like us, or us like them. Their fat button noses, hand-like paws and pleasantly pudgy forms endear beavers to us in a way no ungulate ever could. Young beavers were held in their godparents' arms. Their quiet ways stirred protective paternal emotions. They were like 'frightened children' in their shipping crates.[6] Baptizing a muskox might smack of mockery, but as the childlike beavers underwent a blessed dip into the Swedish waters they cleansed past wrongs, brought sight to environmental blindness, and healed an emotional rift between humans and the once hunted beasts.

A veterinarian examines Norwegian beavers before their introduction into the Swedish landscape, 1922.

We are far more likely to preserve what we know and to protect what we can see. Even in Canada, a nation which upholds the beaver as its national icon, most citizens are far more likely to know beavers from representations on a nickel or a national brand than to have seen the living animal. It takes a patient observer with a sharp eye at dusk to spot a beaver gliding through the water. Beaver charms are elusive, and it is hardly surprising that Grey Owl gained international attention in the 1930s by simply capturing moving images of his beavers on film.

Between 1928 and Grey Owl's death in 1938, the Dominion Parks produced seven films featuring Grey Owl and his beavers, three of which were edited and re-released with sound. The strength of the films, and of Grey Owl's message, rested squarely on the charms of Jelly Roll and Rawhide, two beavers Grey Owl and Anahareo tamed after McGinnis and McGinty disappeared into the wilderness. As icons of the Canadian woods, Jelly Roll and Rawhide could hardly have been more endearing, or Grey Owl more paternalistic. Paddling silently across the lake, calling his beavers from his canoe and tipping it slightly so they could scramble in, Grey Owl acted as a wise and patient father to his rambunctious furry children.

Tamed is not quite the right word. McGinnis and McGinty vanished at some point between the publication of Grey Owl's first and second magazine articles. Aware that his new persona depended on his relationship with beavers, Grey Owl determined to find new companions. In *Pilgrims of the Wild* (1935) he wrote that it was Dave, an Algonquin whom he and Anahareo had befriended, who initiated the plan. 'We can't get along without beaver now,' Dave apparently said, 'we must get some more.' So Anahareo and Dave set off 25 miles into the woods to look for more beaver kits. They found a lodge with four young ones, and took two tiny beavers that weighed but 85 g (3 oz) each. 'By rights

they were too young to have been taken', Grey Owl wrote. (Grey Owl absolved himself of blame as he had been unable to make the trip due to illness.) One kit died. The other became sick and huddled in her box in misery and pain. Yet she survived to become the famous Jelly Roll, starlet of the Dominion Parks films. Rawhide's entry into Grey Owl's family was less stage-managed. He had been badly wounded in a trap and was nursed back to health.

Financed by the Canadian government, the films sparked a nationalistic pride, as well as an international interest, in beaver conservation. The bond between Grey Owl and his beavers as played out on film had a transformative power. The relationship was meant to inspire viewers to refresh and rekindle their own relationships with wild places, to step back from the demands of an increasingly urban existence and reconnect with nature – if not physically then at least spiritually and emotionally. Within Grey Owl's message,

> Beaver stood for something vital, something essential in this wilderness, were a component part of it, they *were* the wilderness. With them gone it would be empty; without them it would be not a wilderness but a waste.[7]

Although the much-hunted beaver, devastated by centuries of greed and vanity, was the natural choice as Grey Owl's totem animal, he could have lived alongside any number of forest crea-tures – squirrels, porcupines, deer or even a young moose, and any of those animals could have marked out a corner for them-selves within his cabin. But Jelly Roll and Rawhide went one step better. They built their lodge half inside, half outside of Grey Owl's cabin. In one film, viewers see Grey Owl seated at his table while, just a few feet away, a beaver pushes a load of mud

The beaver logo of manufacturing company Roots Canada is meant to convey an authentically Canadian idea of nature.

Beavers working on their lodge inside Grey Owl's cabin, Prince Albert National Park.

and twigs up into the cabin and busily pats it all in place. Physically blurring the divide between a human space within and the animal wildness without, the beavers and their lodge embodied the paradoxical image of a domesticated wilderness. They implicitly suggested that 'wild' places needed to be managed and monitored in order to survive, a vision that likely informed Parks Canada's decision to use the beaver as its icon.

Jelly Roll and Rawhide offer a counterpoint to that other wilderness icon, the wolf. Within most western cultures, wolves have traditionally been represented as haunting and savage, travelling in predatory packs – the animal embodiment of the terrifying powers of wild places beyond human control. As Garry Marvin explains in *Wolf*, such a representation depends on a notion of human spaces set apart. By domesticating livestock and demarcating the physical and cultural boundaries of home, humans set up a troubled relationship between the protected, domesticated sphere within, and the dangerous, intruding forces that live 'out there' in the wilds. Wolves are wildness made flesh and blood.

But beavers have never been truly wild within human imaginings because, for millennia, they primarily lived within the imagination. They were too scarce to be seen, let alone to intrude upon and threaten human property. And besides, beavers have always stood for all that is good and worthy. From a classical symbol of austerity and chastity, to furry capital and the animal embodiment of cooperation and industry, beavers have always been valued and admired. In turn, as symbols of Canadian conservation, cast as lost children of the woods, Grey Owl's cinematic beavers were heart-warming, endearing and nostalgic, and entwined the wilderness and all its animals into a soulful and vulnerable whole.

The updated Parks Canada beaver logo.

Montréal 1976

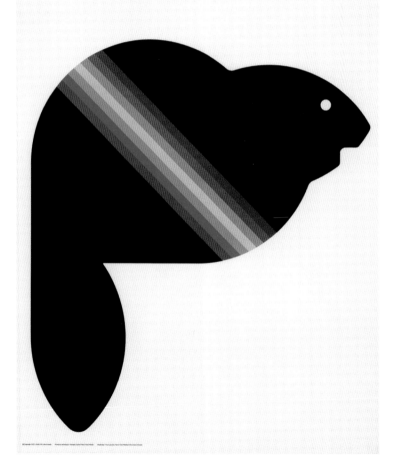

Inspired by Grey Owl's beaver conservation, Dorothy Richards established Beaversprite, a wildlife sanctuary in the Adirondack Mountains, in the 1930s.

Almost a century has passed since *The Beaver People* was filmed, and beavers have, once again, metamorphosed. Although the 1930s in North America were stricken by a decade-long drought, Grey Owl's beavers were icons of wilderness preservation, not wetland protection. But recently, largely thanks to a growing understanding of the environmental benefits of healthy wetlands and the animals' ever-growing numbers, beavers are now seen as highly skilled (some might say unrelenting) wetland specialists and riparian rehabilitators. From wild places to wet places, from childlike victims to tireless agents of ecological transformation, beavers finally enter the twenty-first century.

Beavers are not simply builders. By feeling trees, flooding an area and retaining stagnant water, they create wetland oases. And by changing the landscape's ecology, beaver craftsmanship directly controls the availability of resources for other organisms. In fact,

Amik (meaning beaver in the Algonquin language) was the mascot of the 1976 Summer Olympics in Montreal.

177

biologists call beavers keystone species, or ecological engineers, for their critical role in creating and sustaining ecosystems.

Amphibians and aquatic insects prefer the still or slow-moving water in beaver ponds, and the silt accumulation at the bottom provides ideal spawning grounds for golden trout. Fallen and decaying trees, either taken down by beavers or killed by flooding, are havens for insects and the birds and animals that eat them. Beaver wetlands are associated with more diverse and abundant bird communities, suggesting beavers could be an important tool for reversing the decline in bird numbers. Studies have also shown that ice melts as much as ten days earlier in beaver ponds, which makes them welcoming habitats for waterfowl, particularly as beaver lodges are prime nesting sites, safely surrounded by protective moats.

Beaver activity can also adversely affect certain species. Many species of fish, for example, cannot survive in the low oxygen levels of stagnant water, and dams can block spawning salmon and other migrating fishes.[8] Beavers' selective wood harvesting reduces the diversity of tree species and can permanently change varied woodlands into a grove of evergreens. However, although beavers deter certain species, by creating niche habitats and attracting different species from those that previously inhabited the area, beavers and their wetlands increase the overall species diversity of the area, a phenomenon known as 'patchiness'. And such beaver patchiness may have a significant global impact.

In 2002 Glynnis Hood conducted doctorate research on the relationship between beaver populations and open water in the Canadian prairies. She compared 54 years of data extending back to the late 1940s, including beaver censuses, rainfall records and historical aerial photographs that showed the extent of open water. The summer of her research turned out to be the driest year on record, and many of the lakes and ponds Hood hoped to study shrank significantly or dried up altogether. The drought would have put an end to her research if beavers were not so good in a crisis.

According to precipitation records, 1950 was the fourth driest year on record, but it still had 47 per cent more rainfall than 2002. However, aerial photographs revealed that the landscape in 1950 had 61 per cent less open water than in 2002. The findings seemed inexplicable until Hood looked at her beaver data. Beavers were mostly absent from the area in the 1950s. By the late twentieth century, they were thriving. In other words, beavers were responsible for keeping water on the land and mitigating the worst effects of the drought.

Because sufficient water stores are essential for their survival, beavers will do everything in their power to ensure their ponds are always deep enough to escape predators. They dredge the bottom of their ponds, particularly around the lodge entrance, and dig a network of canals to collect and direct any available water into their ponds. Hood also found that lakes with active beaver dams were deeper and had nine times more water than those without, even during drought. Often ranchers' only access to water was a beaver pond. The evidence was clear: beavers increased the land's resilience to dramatic climatic events. 'A world without beavers', Hood concluded, 'was most evidently a world without water.'[9]

The Aboriginal Nations of the Great Plains also discovered the secrets of beaver hydrology. In the lush, well-watered forests of the northeast coast, the Iroquois and Heron Nations were only too eager to trade beaver skins for European goods. But as fur traders made their way westward into the prairies they reported that the indigenous people, traditionally nomadic bison hunters, refused to kill beavers. Alex Henry, an English fur trader who travelled with an Ojibwe family for a year in the 1760s, noted

that certain tribes of the open Plains 'will not kill a beaver . . . to enable them to purchase an ax or other European utensil, though beaver are numerous in every stream throughout their country'.[10]

Anthropologists have traditionally ascribed the ancient aversion to beaver hunting to the animal's sacred importance among many Nations across the Great Plains. Several tribes from the Blackfoot Nations believed that the world had been made by a giant beaver. Other groups claimed descent from beavers, and the Beaver Bundle was at the centre of the Blackfoot's most sacred ceremonies. Various legends surround the Beaver Bundle's spiritual origins, but most tell of a wandering or forsaken man or woman who is taken in by a beaver. The beaver eventually sends the wanderer back to his or her people with a precious gift: a bundle of objects with healing properties and powerful prayers, dances and songs to defend against death and disease.

In a fascinating study of beavers among several Aboriginal Nations of the Great Plains, Rosalind Grace Morgan has suggested there may be an ecological basis to the beaver's spiritual significance. Water was limited on the prairies, particularly during hot summer months, and knowing the locations of beaver dams and ponds could be a matter of survival. Also, beavers provided humans with easy access to firewood and construction materials. As bison

Ojibwe chief's pouch made of beaver skin, calico and beads.

A series of beaver dams and ponds on McClure Pass, Colorado.

During his entire trip up the Missouri river in 1843, the great nature illustrator John James Audubon never saw a single beaver.

was abundantly available for meat and fur, beavers were far more valuable for their water conservation and resource management. On a hard landscape cracked by long drought, the life-giving powers of water surely ran through the symbolism of the healing beaver.[11]

As white settlements expanded westwards across the North American continent, a hundred million acres of wetlands, long considered unwholesome and unproductive, were drained for agriculture and urban use. As Hood points out, 'The landscapes of North America and Europe coevolved with the beaver, and without it their ecology goes awry.'[12] Would the catastrophic droughts of the 1930s, which turned the prairies into a giant dust bowl, or the Civil War Drought of the 1850s and '60s, which accelerated the near-extinction of the bison, have been less severe if beavers and their wetlands had still been plentiful? Perhaps. Perhaps not. But the answers to history may lie in the future.

At the end of the nineteenth century, American wildlife agents began live-trapping beavers from isolated pockets and relocating them into their former habitats. No beavers had been seen in the State of Pennsylvania since 1903. Between 1915 and 1924, 47 pairs were imported. By 1934 those 94 beavers had become 15,000. In 1935, Grey Owl's Prince Albert National Park had only about 500 beavers. By the 1940s, wardens were relocating the animals into beaver-barren parks across the country, including Wood Buffalo National Park, which is now home to the world's largest-known beaver dam. And in one of the strangest acts of conservation, in 1948 the Idaho's fish and Game Department air-dropped 76 beavers, in crates equipped with parachutes, into prime beaver forests.

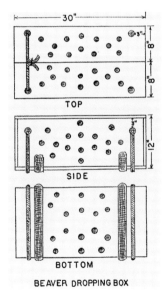

The model for the boxes used to airdrop beavers. The crates were rigged to open on impact.

With the exception of only one casualty, all the beavers were transplanted successfully. Beavers now occupy most of their traditional territory including – most improbably – the Bronx River in New York City. Current estimates put North America's beaver population at around 15 million to 25 million.

Eurasian beavers are thriving as well. Latvia, Sweden and Russia were the first countries to begin rehabilitating their populations in the 1920s. Germany and Finland followed in the 1930s. Latvia, Lithuania and Poland introduced beavers in the 1940s. Over the following decades, beavers were introduced throughout their native range, from the British Isles to Mongolia. By and large the animals have all been transplanted successfully and show no signs of decline. In 1997, the continent's beaver population reached 400,000. Five years later, that number jumped to 600,000. In 2012, beavers were estimated to be 1 million strong.

But not all returning beavers are welcome. For starters, not all of Eurasia's beavers are Eurasian. Early twentieth-century introductions of North American beavers into Europe and Russia have never been fully eradicated. Of the Finnish population, for example, 90 per cent are descended from seven North American beavers released in 1937. Then again, even some Eurasian beavers are proving undesirable. A family of wild beavers was unexpectedly spotted in 2014 on the River Otter in Devonshire, in the southwest tip of England. The landowner captured video footage of the family with infra-red cameras and posted it online. These were the first wild beavers seen in Britain since before the time of Gerald of Wales. But the beavers' midnight antics did not amuse George Eustice, a minister at the Department for Environment, Food and Rural Affairs. In a written parliamentary address in 2014, Eustice outlined that the government intended to capture the beavers and place them in a zoo. 'They could be carrying a disease not currently present in the UK', he wrote. 'In addition,

beavers have not been an established part of our wildlife for the last 500 years. Our landscape and habitats have changed since then and we need to assess the impact they could have.'[13] (As the landowner is currently happy with the beavers, some critics suggest Eustice is being pressured by local angling societies.) Although a Scottish trial is currently under way to re-establish Eurasian beavers (imported from Norway), the European Union's current acute anxiety over invasive species has transformed returning beavers into suspicious invaders. Local wildlife groups have rallied around the beavers with the hope of forestalling their removal. Action has yet to be taken.

Living with beavers is not just a matter of letting beavers loose. Aside from humans, few animals have the power to transform

In 2009, 16 Norwegian beavers were introduced into Scotland as part of a 5-year trial to determine whether such introductions would be beneficial to Scottish nature conservation.

environments as radically as beavers, and not surprisingly, the two species do not always share the same landscape design.

The truth is, beavers and humans have never really cohabitated. As medieval towns grew into cities, beavers were driven into extinction through most of Europe. Before Europeans arrived in North America, the vast continent offered sufficient geography for humans and beavers to pursue parallel lives relatively unhindered. And once Europeans did arrive, settlement followed the fur trade, which is to say, trappers and traders had already depleted beaver populations before homesteaders began clearing the land.

Since beavers were last abundant, modern cities have sprawled across the landscape. Roads and highways, railway lines, sewer systems and housing developments crisscross what was once prime beaver territory, which means humans and beavers are forced to coexist in ways that are not altogether agreeable for either species.

Each year, the average adult beaver cuts approximately one metric tonne of wood – about 215 trees – for food and building materials. With tens of millions of beavers hard at work, beavers do tens of millions of dollars' worth of damage to human property and urban infrastructure. Beavers dam up culverts and irrigation ditches. They flood roads, inundate septic systems and destroy hay meadows and croplands. They take down ornamental trees and turn city parks into marshlands. Even within nature reserves far from urban centres, wardens are often tasked with eliminating beavers that dam up drainage systems. By cutting down mature trees, beavers cause soil erosion and endanger the stability of roadways and underpasses. In 1984 a train travelling between Washington DC and Montreal derailed after a flood from a broken beaver dam washed out the railway embankment. Five people were killed. In Poland, beavers are partly blamed for the

2013 floods that killed fifteen people: they had burrowed through the levees along the Vistula River, weakening flood defences. Beavers have also burrowed through parts of the Netherlands' famous dyke system, which protects a high percentage of the country from being overwhelmed by the North Sea.

The virtues of beaver industry can quickly be relabelled as the vices of an unrelenting rodent, particularly when beavers are undeterred by repeated evictions, relocations, and dam and

A tree wrapped with wire mesh to prevent further damage.

lodge destruction. The sound of running water sends beavers into urgent repair mode, which means as soon as beavers hear water running through an unplugged culvert or broken dam, they spring into action. Farmers can dynamite a dam to save their crops, only to find the dam rebuilt overnight. Trapping and relocating is only a temporary cure; if one family of beavers considers the area agreeable, likely as not another family will soon move into the empty pond.

Such remorseless industry prompted Canadian Senator Nancy Eaton to call for polar bears to replace beavers as Canada's national symbols. In a 2011 Senate speech, Eaton called the beaver a 'dentally defective rat' and a 'toothy tyrant'. Her low opinion of the animals seems to have arisen from a personal grudge against a beaver family that, despite relocations and dam demolitions, doggedly continued to do damage to her cottage in rural Ontario.

Every morning, wardens in Vancouver's Stanley Park remove the branches and mud beavers have plugged into the culvert; this wall of debris had been 5 years in the making.

Far from a model of industry, and despite its importance in Canadian history, the beaver had become 'a nuisance that wreaks havoc on farmlands, roads, lakes, streams and tree plantations, including my dock every summer'.[14]

Eaton's comment sparked a wry national discussion, and although the beaver remained unthreatened as Canada's emblem, a group of Ontario farmers used the debate as an opportunity to declare war on beavers. Over the past 30 years, as beavers resurged in numbers, their farmlands were slowly becoming swamps. One farmer had lost more than half his 57-acre sheep farm to flooding caused by beavers along a stretch of creek. But trapping and relocating beavers or breaching their dams was a losing battle. With a touch of poetic justice for the fur trade, no matter what farmers did to rid themselves of the animals, waves of beavers kept coming. 'It's a war', one of the farmers declared, 'It's really a war.'[15]

One American group has a very different opinion on the matter. In 2006, two beavers moved into Alhambra Creek in downtown Martinez, California, a town formerly best known as the home and final resting place of the naturalist John Muir. The beavers built a dam 9 m (30 ft) wide and 1.8 m (6 ft) high, and chewed through half of the trees recently planted by the city as part of a $9.7 million improvement project. The city council declared the beavers a nuisance and a flooding hazard, and the animals were slated for extermination. However, many of the townspeople wanted the beavers to stay, and after much debate, the townspeople won.

But if humans want to cohabit with beavers, it is humans who will have to adapt, not beavers. Living with beavers takes work, particularly in urban areas. If left unchecked, beaver dams will continue to grow and flood ever-larger areas. As Alhambra Creek runs right through the centre of town, Martinez's beavers

The cut tail identifies the beaver as Mom beaver, one of the original pair at Martinez.

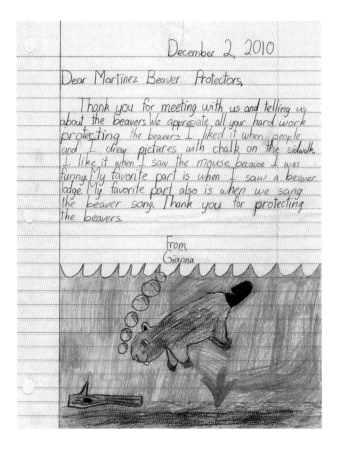

December 2, 2010

Dear Martinez Beaver Protectors,

Thank you for meeting with us and telling us about the beavers. We appreciate all your hard work protecting the beavers. I liked it when people and I drew pictures with chalk on the sidewalk. I like it when I saw the mouse, because I was funny. My favorite part is when I saw a beaver lodge. My favorite part also is when we sang the beaver song. Thank you for protecting the beavers.

From,
Gianna

were going to require diligent management if the project was to succeed.

The beaver advocates formed a committee to manage the animals and sought the advice of Skip Lisle, the Vermont biologist and inventor of flow-control devices including the aptly named Beaver Deceiver™ and Castor Master™. Simply put, such devices allow a controlled amount of water to flow through a dam or culvert (thereby releasing surplus water which might cause flooding and damage to human property) without the beavers' knowledge.

Fooling beavers is a tricky challenge, and to be successful a flow-control device must eliminate the sound and feel of running water. Most systems involve a large fencing structure, a flexible pipe, or both. A Beaver Deceiver is a trapezoidal-shaped fence, often combined with a hollow pipe, mainly used to keep culverts clear of debris and running freely. A Castor Master, which Lisle installed in Alhambra Creek, controls the height of the water with a large flexible tube that covertly drains the water and prevents dams from growing vertically. The inlet of the pipe is enclosed within a fence which masks the sound and feel of the escaping water at the intake. With their Castor Master installed and the water levels under control, the beaver advocates of Martinez have established the non-profit organization Worth a Dam, dedicated to inspiring and educating other urban communities on the ecological and community benefits of co-existing with beavers.

A flexible pond leveller being installed.

Beaver dam and pond studded with dead trees in Eastern Sierra, California.

As fears of a changing climate loom large in the twenty-first century, the beaver's powers over water are once again transforming the animal into a role model, if not a saviour. Beaver believers, as they call themselves, believe that the worst effects of unpredictable weather patterns and droughts might be assuaged by beavers' water management. Run-off of melting snow surges down from the mountains, flash-flooding the land, and is usually long gone before the dry summer months. But beaver dams retain and slow water, giving it time to soak into the ground so it can nourish the soil and sustain plant and animal life. Beaver ponds store rainfall and beaver canals are natural irrigation ditches. By retaining water, beavers keep more water on the land throughout the seasons and moderate the impact of both flooding and drought. Moreover, healthy riparian habitats improve the quality of river water, elevate the water table and increase the open water available for livestock and wildlife.

Those dramatic benefits have encouraged many ecologists to see beavers as a cost-effective means of enhancing the vitality and resilience of the landscape. The state of Washington is currently studying beavers as an alternative to a proposed $10 billion concrete reservoir. The Grand Canyon Trust is re-establishing beaver populations in Utah in the hope of rehabilitating wetlands throughout the state. And in Ulaanbaatar, beavers are restoring the headwaters of the Tuul River. After the breakup of communism left many Mongolians hunting for survival, beaver populations dwindled and so did the wetlands. A 2003 study revealed that 22 of 72 tributaries of the Tuul had dried up. As 60 per cent of Mongolians live along the Tuul and rely on its water supply, the government has allocated one billion tugriks (about $740,000) to restore nature's hydraulic engineer and coax the river systems back to health. In 2012, 44 beavers were live-trapped in Germany and Russia and sent to Mongolia.

As beavers resurge in extraordinary numbers, humans have at last been forced to see them as evolutionarily perfected agents of ecological change, and not amalgamations of peculiar parts. Living with beavers means learning to see the animals as masterful builders and learning to manage their environmental impact. Whether beavers disturb or enhance the nature we hope to curate, our relationship with the ecological beaver is bound to be complicated, unpredictable and perhaps even a little messy. Coexistence is possible, and allowing beavers to take an active role in wetland management may be beneficial not just for humans and beavers, but for the health of the planet.

But of course a darkness lurks within every beaver romance, and the ecological beaver is not exempt. As beavers are being heralded as climate change heroes in the northern hemisphere, the third continental wave of beaver obliteration is being planned at the bottom of the world. Ironically, the impeding cull is motivated precisely by the fact that beavers are such phenomenal agents of ecological transformation.

In 1946, 50 North American beavers, trapped in Canada, were let loose on Isla Grande at the southern tip of South America's archipelago. The plan was to start a fur trade in the largely uninhabited and rugged terrain. The fur trade floundered, and the beavers were left unchecked for decades. Without any predators, they quickly spread through their exotic environment and now inhabit nearly all streams and aquatic habitats in the archipelago,

Beaver damage in Tierra del Fuego National Park, Argentina.

and have even been seen on the mainland. The beaver population is estimated to be 200,000 and growing.

Patagonia's ecology did not evolve to support beavers. The riparian forests of the region mainly consist of three species of beech trees in the genus *Nothofagus*. All three species are eaten by beavers, only one can survive in marshlands, and all struggle to regrow in soil disturbed by beavers. *Nothofagus* regenerates by seed banks, but beaver flooding and foraging drown and damage the seedling, severely affecting the trees' ability to regenerate. In contrast, aspen, one of the beaver's preferred trees in North America, typically grow in large clonal colonies and spread by means of root suckers. By taking down a tree, beavers have not killed the plant but simply pruned a shoot of an ancient root system. But southern beech do not regenerate, forcing beavers to move ever-forward into new territories to take down yet more trees. Also, while beaver wetlands in the northern hemisphere increase the overall diversity of the environment, the same is not true in South America. The plants inhabiting beaver meadows in Patagonia are the same species that grow in other non-forested environments. In fact, it seems that invasive plants are far more likely to grow once *Nothofagus* is removed.

Argentina first tried to control beavers by issuing hunting licences in 1981, and Chile officially recognized beavers as a harmful species in 1992. Both governments encouraged commercial trapping. When the fur market stagnated, they began paying a bounty on beaver tails delivered to local authorities. A few intrepid restaurateurs even explored the possibilities of beaver cuisine, but with little success. No one was keen to eat beaver.

In the effort to right past environmental wrongs, in 2008 Argentina and Chile signed a bi-national agreement to eradicate every beaver within their nations' territorial limits. The extermination is estimated to take at least nine years, cost $35 million,

For a time, a bounty was paid to beaver hunters in Tierra del Fuego.

and will use helicopters to fly from island to island over an area roughly 160,000 km² (40 million acres) in size. In an interview with *Nature*, ecologist Josh Donlan, director of Advanced Conservation Strategies, described the process like war, echoing Canadian farmers: 'We'll have to move in on the beavers in a rolling front', he said, 'going from watershed to watershed to remove them, with a massive monitoring programme behind to make sure they have all been eradicated.'[16]

A similarly massive effort was mounted against goats on the Galapagos Islands. Like the Tierra del Fuego beavers, the introduced goats multiplied enthusiastically and, without any predators, devastated the islands' native flora and fauna. When their numbers reached 80,000, a team of conservationists and scientists initiated a four-and-a-half-year eradication programme that cost

$6 million and succeeded in hunting down every last goat. The team even used 'Mata Hari' goats – sterilized females in chemically induced heat – to lure the last males out of hiding.[17]

With 200,000 animals slated for extermination, the Tierra del Fuego beavers will be the largest mammal population ever to be purposefully and systematically eliminated from a territory. The Austral Centre of Scientific Investigations is encouraging the tourist industry to stop advertising beaver-spotting as a tourist attraction and to avoid cute beavers in their logos.

For much of the twentieth century, humans have lamented the millennia of beaver slaughter across the northern hemisphere. But the fur trade never aimed to exterminate beavers, and it is a strange twist of fate that at precisely the moment beavers are heralded as climate change heroes and wetland saviours, the first planned beaver eradication programme is set to commence.

After befriending a family of beavers on her wildness property in Atlantic County, New Jersey, Hope Sawyer Buyukmihci founded The Beaver Defenders in 1970, an organization dedicated to beaver protection.

Is Patagonia's unique and fragile ecosystem more important to preserve than nearly a quarter of a million displaced beavers? Perhaps. But the ethical challenge posed by the slaughter rests on the simple fact that beavers are not like other invasive species. Rats, goats, rabbits, pigs and other unwanted and destructive introduced species are either displaced domesticated animals or ancient pests. They have never been endangered. They have never shaped the contours of empires or symbolized a fragile wildness of a nation. But beavers are Rawhide and Jelly Roll. They were baptized by Swedish waters. They are Canada's official emblem and parables of industry and ingenuity. They are wetland rehabilitators who – by an ill-advised fur infatuation – were dislocated from their home territory with devastating effect.

Beaver appreciation and beaver obliteration have never been mutually exclusive. We have always loved beavers to death. The unsettling events at the bottom of the world should remind us that we have also loved our ideas of beaver into oblivion. There is no cultural remembrance of Aesop's beaver as a model of chastity and austerity. Few histories appreciate what made beaver pelts so precious – just one fur in a land teeming with bear, lynx, muskrats, bison and fox. Even in Canada, the hundred-strong beaver work force has utterly disappeared from the national imagination. And the remarkable recovery of beavers within the last 50 years has erased almost all memory that beavers were once on the brink of extinction. The beaver's exceptional parts and unique capabilities have inspired an extraordinarily varied poetic and material richness, which also means beavers are easily discarded. Once a beaver loses relevance, there are always others to take its place.

The animal embodiment of austerity, prudence, industry, wealth, cooperation, ingenuity, instinct, intelligence, freedom, wild spaces and ecological rehabilitation, beavers have always reflected what humans desire the most. But as happens sometimes with

obsessions, the real beaver all but disappears within narratives that reveal far more about our human desires and aspirations than the lives of beavers. And in that, our long and lusty beaver romances offer a few words of warning, advice, and perhaps even a little hope. It will always be hard to see a beaver, but learning the skill may teach us to see ourselves, our infatuations and our follies more clearly.

Performance artist Christy Gast imagines the beaver's experience in Tierra el Fuego: *Beaver Crossing the Beagle Channel,* 2014.

Timeline of the Beaver

c. 54 million years ago	*c.* 23 million years ago	8–7.6 million years ago	620–520 BC
The earliest beaver-like animals diverge from their closest ancestor	Fossil evidence suggests *Steneofiber eseri* was the earliest woodcutting and swimming castorid	Migration over the Beringia land bridge initiates speciation between *Castor canadenis* and *Castor fiber*	Aesop's Fables include 'The Beaver and his Testicles'

1670	1758	1820	1825	1827
Hudson's Bay Company grants a fur monopoly on a 3.9 million sq. km (1.5 million sq. mile) watershed	Carl Linnaeus places beavers and the Russian desman in the genus *Castor*	Heinrich Kuhl classifies North American beavers as a separate species	The first Rocky Mountain Rendezvous is held for trappers to sell their furs	François-René de Chateaubriand describes beaver villages as the 'Venice of the wilderness'

1937	1946	1952	1957	1973	1975
North American beavers introduced to Finland	North American beavers introduced to Tierra del Fuego	Canadian park wardens begin lethal trapping in Grey Owl's Prince Albert National Park to keep populations in check	The American television series *Leave it to Beaver* debuts	Chromosomal testing finally confirms *Castor canadensis* and *Castor fiber* as separate species	The beaver attains official status as Canada's emblem

4th century BC	29 BC	7th century AD	1188	1598
Hippocrates recommends castoreum for gynaecological distresses	Virgil describes Pontus on the Turkish coast of the Black Sea as the origin of 'rank' castoreum	Anglo-Saxons wear beaver-tooth pendants as amulets to protect against toothache	Gerald of Wales claims the River Teifi has the last beaver colony in Great Britain	North America's first fur-trading post established at Île de Sable

1836	1845	1922	1927	1928
First beaver sanctuary established by the Hudson's Bay Company on Charlton Island	Norway passes Europe's earliest beaver protection law	John Kettlewell publishes *Beaver*, an instructional handbook on beard-spotting	*Oxford English Dictionary* records the first recorded use of 'beaver' as sexual slang for the female genitalia	Beavers first appear on film in Grey Owl's *The Beaver People*

1986	1990s	2004	2008	2013
Beaver Scouts introduced by the Scout Association	Skip Lisle invents the Beaver Deceiver and Castor Master	Beaverlodge, Alberta, installs a 1,350-kg (3,000-lb) beaver sculpture as part of the town's 75th anniversary	Chile and Argentina sign a binational agreement to eradicate beavers from Tierra del Fuego	A man in Belarus dies after being bitten by a beaver

Glossary

A quick reference to the many beavers and their parts.

bank beaver, n., a beaver that burrows into a river bank rather than building a lodge. Bank beavers were long thought to be a separate species from lodge-building beavers.

bark stones, n., *see* **beaver stones**

beaver, n., a large amphibious rodent with webbed feet, a broad flat tail and strong architectural inclinations;

a hat made from felted beaver underfur. Also known as bever;

the visor or lower portion of a helmet. When the ghost of Hamlet's father appeared in full battle armour, Horatio knew it was the old king because 'he wore his beaver up';

a light afternoon snack, usually at 3 o'clock;

a single-engined propeller-driven bush plane made by de Havilland Canada and synonymous with the Canadian wilderness;

a five- to eight-year-old in the youngest section of the Scout Association;

a beard.

sexual slang for the female genitalia.

beaver, v., to work energetically. Also, as busy as a beaver, to work like a beaver.

beaver believer, n., an American beaver champion who believes that beaver wetlands will mitigate the worst effects of climate change.

Beaver Deceiver, n., a trapezoidal-shaped fence invented by Skip Lisle to keep culverts clear of beaver debris.

Beaver Defenders, n., a beaver protection and education group founded by Hope Buyukmihci in 1970.

beaver fever, n., a popular name for the parasitic disease giardiasis. The name originated after 140 cases of giardiasis were traced to a reservoir inhabited by infected beavers.

beaver intellect, n., a plodding yet honest mentality.

beaver leaver, n., a male homosexual.

beaver shot, n., a pornographic picture of a woman's genitals.

beaver stones, n., a beaver's castor sacs, so called because the scent organs were long believed to be the animal's testicles, or stones. The castor sacs were also known as bark stones, as they contained what looked like finely pulverized bark.

beaver tail, n., a deep-fried sweetbread.

buck, n., a coin issued by the Hudson's Bay Company that equalled the value of one beaver pelt. *See also* **made beaver**

castoreum, n., the yellowish secretion of a beaver's castor sac which, in combination with beaver urine, is used in territorial scent marking. Also known as castor.

Castor, twin brother of Pollux in Greek and Roman mythology and collectively known as the *Dioskouroi*. Castor's connection to beavers is unknown.

Castor canadensis, n., the North American beaver.

Castor fiber, n., the Eurasian beaver.

castor-gras, n., beaver skins unpicked from a North American aboriginal's winter beaver robe. Also known as **greasy beaver**.

Castor Master, n., a flow-control device invented by Skip Lisle to drain water from the beaver dam.

castor sacs, n., a beaver's scent organs used in territorial marking.

castor sec, n., a beaver skin stretched and dried on hooped branches. Also known as **dry beaver** or parchment.

dry beaver, n., *see* **castor sec**

greasy beaver, n., *see* **castor-gras**

in beaver, v., to be in non-academic dress, that is, to wear a tall beaver hat rather than an academic cap and gown.

made beaver, n., unit of currency used by the Hudson's Bay Company equivalent to one beaver pelt. *See also* **buck**

References

INTRODUCTION

1 Samuel Pepys, *The Diary of Samuel Pepys*, ed. Henry Morley (New York, 1900), p. 169.
2 Thomas Douglas Selkirk, *A Sketch of the British Fur Trade in North America* (London, 1816), p. 25.

1 BEAVER

1 Cromwell Mortimer, 'The Anatomy of a Female Beaver, and an Account of the Castor Found in Her', *Philosophical Transactions*, XXXVIII (1733), pp. 180–82.
2 Giraldus Cambrensis, *The Itinerary Through Wales* (London, 1935), p. 106.
3 Michael Drayton, 'Poly-Olbion, Song VI', *The Complete Works of Michael Drayton*, ed. Richard Hooper (London, 1876), vol. 1, p. 149.
4 Mortimer, 'The Anatomy', p. 174.
5 Pliny the Elder, *The Natural History*, trans. John Bostock and H. T. Riley (London, 1855), vol. II, p. 297.
6 Peter Andrea Mathiolus, *Commentaires sur les six livres de Ped. Dioscoride*, trans. Jean de Moulines (Lyon, 1572), p. 213.
7 Bridget Ann Henisch, *Fast and Feast: Food in Medieval Society* (University Park, PA, 1976), p. 47.
8 Charles Wilson, 'Notes on the Prior Existence of *Castor fiber* in Scotland, with its Ancient and Present Distribution in Europe, and on the Use of Castoreum', *Edinburgh New Philosophical Journal*, VIII (1858), p. 28.

9 Bartholomaeus Anglicus, *De proprietatibus rerum*, trans. John Tervisa (London, 1535), p. 324, verso.

10 Georges-Louis Leclerc, Comte de Buffon, *Buffon's Natural History*, trans. J. S. Barr [1797] (London, 1807), vol. VI, p. 50.

11 Pliny, *The Natural History*, pp. 297–8.

12 John Guillim, *A Display of Heraldrie: Manifesting a More Easie Accesse to the Knowledge Thereof Then Hath Beene Hitherto Published by Any* (London, 1611), p. 178.

13 William Wood, *New England's Prospect* [1634] (Boston, MA, 1865), p. 28.

14 François-Marc Gagnon, *Images du Castor Canadien XVIe–XVIIIe siècles* (Quebec, 1994), p. 57.

15 Mortimer, 'The Anatomy,' pp. 179–80.

16 Claude Perrault, *Description Anatomique, d'un Cameleon, d'un Castor, d'un Dromadaire, d'un Ours, et d'une Gazelle* (Paris, 1669), p. 51.

17 Glynnis Hood, *The Beaver Manifesto* (Victoria, 2011), p. 9.

18 Natalia Rybczynski, 'Castorid Phylogenetics: Implications for the Evolution of Swimming and Tree-Exploitation in Beavers', *Journal of Mammalian Evolution*, XIV/1 (2007), pp. 1–35, 12.

19 Dietland Müller-Schwarze, *The Beaver: Its Life and Impact*, 2nd edn (Ithaca, NY, 2011), p. 11.

2 MUSK

1 William Alexander, *Experimental Essays* (Oxford, 1768), p. 83.

2 J.C.G. Jörg, 'Medical Experiments,' *The London Medical Gazette* XXVI (1840), p. 952.

3 John Eberle, *A Treatise on the Materia Medica and Therapeutics*, 6th edn (Philadelphia, PA, 1847), p. 415.

4 Aesop, 'The Beaver and his Testicles', *Aesop's Fables*, trans. Laura Gibbs (Oxford, 2002), p. 207.

5 Moyse Charas, *Histoire naturelle des animaux, des plantes et des minéraux qui entrent dans la composition de la Thériaque d'andromachus* (Paris, 1668), p. 248.

6 Anya H. King, 'The Musk Trade and the Near East in the Early
   Medieval Period', PhD dissertation, University of Indiana, 2007,
   pp. 27–9.

7 Pliny the Elder, *The Natural History of Pliny*, trans. John Bostock
   and H. T. Riley (London, 1857), vol. VI, p. 13.

8 Ibid., p. 13.

9 Leonardo da Vinci, *The Notebooks of Leonardo da Vinci*,
   ed. Jean Paul Richter, trans. R. C. Bell (New York, 1970),
   pp. 325, 323, 316.

10 Aesop, 'The Hunted Beaver', *The Fables of Aesop with a Life of the
    Author*, ed. Samuel Croxall (London, 1793), vol. I, p. 79.

11 Juvenal, *The Sixteen Satires of Juvenal*, trans. S. H. Jeyes (Oxford,
    1885), p. 165.

12 Aelian, *On the Characteristics of Animals*, trans. A. F. Scholfield,
    3 vols (London, 1959), vol. II, p. 51.

13 Andrea Alciato, 'Emblem 153', *Emblematum liber*, trans.
    William Barker and Jean Guthrie, www.mun/ca/alciato,
    2 October 2013.

14 *Physiologus: A Medieval Book of Nature Lore*, trans. Michael J. Curley
    (Chicago, 2009), p. 52.

15 Aesop, 'The Hunted Beaver', p. 79.

16 George A. Burdock, *Fenaroli's Handbook of Flavor Ingredients*,
    5th edn (Boca Raton, FL, 2005), p. 277.

17 G. A. Burdock, 'Safety Assessment of Castoreum Extract as a
    Food Ingredient', *International Journal of Toxicology*, XXVI/1
    (2007), p. 55.

18 Lucretius, *The Nature of Things*, trans. Frank O. Copley
    (New York, 1977), p. 165.

19 Robert Griffith Eglesfeld, *A Universal Formulary: Containing the
    Methods of Preparing and Administering Officinal and Other
    Medicines* (Philadelphia, PA, 1850), p. 151.

20 John Redman Coxe, *The American Dispensatory*, 6th edn
    (Philadelphia, PA, 1825), p. 168.

21 Peter Canvane, *A Dissertation on the Oleum Palmæ Christi*
    (Bath, 1766), p. 4.

22 Frank Rosell and Sun Lixing, 'Use of Anal Gland Secretion to Distinguish the Two Beaver Species *Castor canadensis* and *C. fiber*', *Wildlife Biology*, v/2 (1999), pp. 119–23.

23 Baron de Lahontan, *New Voyages to North-America*, ed. Reuben Gold Thwaites [1703] (Chicago, IL, 1905), vol. II, p. 482.

24 Charles Wolley, *A Two Years' Journal in New York* [1701] (Cleveland, OH, 1902), p. 49.

25 John D. Godman, *American Natural History* (Philadelphia, PA, 1826), vol. II, p. 36.

26 Pierre François-Xavier de Charlevoix, *Journal of a Voyage to North America* (London, 1761), vol. I, p. 157.

3 FUR

1 *Old Bailey Proceedings*, October 1686, Edward Newgent; August 1688, John Wyatt; July 1688, George Stockwell, www.oldbaileyonline.org, accessed 17 July 2013.

2 *Old Bailey Proceedings*, October 1687, Cibile Jones; December 1722, Henry Player.

3 *Old Bailey Proceedings*, February 1688, James Jordan.

4 Henry Percival Biggar, ed., *The Voyages of Jacques Cartier* (Toronto, 1993), p. 24.

5 Reuben Gold Thwaites, ed., *The Jesuit Relations and Allied Documents* (Cleveland, OH, 1898), vol. VI, pp. 296–7.

6 Chantal Nadeau, *Fur Nation: From the Beaver to Brigitte Bardot* (New York, 2001), p. 11.

7 Anthony Dent, *Lost Beasts of Britain* (London, 1974), p. 55.

8 Marc Lescarbot, *The History of New France*, trans. W. L. Grant (Toronto, 1914), vol. III, p. 117.

9 Phillip Stubbes, *Anatomy of Abuses in England*, ed. Frederick J. Furnivall (London, 1877–9), pp. 7, 8, 50.

10 Madeleine Ginsburg, *The Hat: Trends and Traditions* (Hauppauge, NY, 1990), p. 44.

11 Glynnis Hood, *The Beaver Manifesto* (Victoria, 2011), p. 22.

12 Adriaen van der Donck, *A Description of New Netherland*, ed.

Charles T. Gehring and William A. Starna, trans. Diederik Willem Goedhuys (Lincoln, NB, 2008), p. 140.

13 Ann M. Carlos and Frank D. Lewis, *Commerce by a Frozen Sea: Native Americans and the European Fur Trade* (Philadelphia, 2010), p. 25.

14 J. T. Crean, 'Hats and the Fur Trade', *Canadian Journal of Economics and Political Science*, XXVIII/3 (1962), p. 380.

15 Eric Jay Dolin, *Fur, Fortune, and Empire: The Epic History of the Fur Trade in America* (New York, 2010), p. 281.

16 *Old Bailey Proceedings*, October 1847, James Saunders.

17 Robert Burns, *The Works of Robert Burns*, ed. Allan Cunningham (London, 1840), p. 396.

18 Aldous Huxley, *Antic Hay* [1923] (New York, 1962), pp. 81, 76.

19 Anonymous, *Immortalia: An Anthology of American Ballads, Sailors' Songs, Cowboy Songs, College Songs, Parodies, Limericks, and Other Humorous Verses and Doggerel* (Alexandria, 1927), p. 166.

20 Huxley, *Antic Hay*, pp. 42–3.

21 Ibid., pp. 35–6.

22 James T. Henke, *Gutter Life and Language in the Early 'Street' Literature of England* (West Cornwall, CT, 1988), p. 22.

23 Francis Grose, *A Classical Dictionary of the Vulgar Tongue* (London, 1931), p. 29.

24 Wendy Coburn, *Beaver Tales*, exh. cat., Oakville Galleries, Ontario (2000), 34.

25 Christopher Dafoe, 'Annals of the Beaver', *The Beaver: Exploring Canada's History*, LXXV/4 (1995), p. 3.

26 William Kingston, *The Western World: Picturesque Sketches of Nature* (London, 1884), p. 123.

4 ARCHITECT

1 Marius Barbeau, *Haida Myths* (Ottawa, 1953), pp. 52–6.

2 James L. Gould and Carol Grant Gould, *Animal Architects: Building and the Evolution of Intelligence* (New York, 2007), p. 251.

3 Nancy Erickson, 'Of Maps and Beavers', www.oshermaps.org,
   2 November 2013.
4 Nicolas Denys, *The Description and Natural History of the Coasts
   of North America* [1672], trans. William F. Ganong (Toronto,
   1908), pp. 92, 363.
5 Ibid., p. 365.
6 Ibid., p. 363.
7 Gerald of Wales, 'The Itinerary Through Wales, and The
   Description of Wales', trans. Richard Colt Hoare, in *The Historical
   Works of Giraldus Cambrensis* (London, 1894), p. 430.
8 William Wood, *New England's Prospect* [1634] (Boston, MA, 1865),
   p. 29.
9 Georges-Louis Leclerc, Comte de Buffon, *Buffon's Natural History*,
   trans. J. S. Barr [1797] (London, 1807), vol. VI, pp. 291, 299.
10 Dièreville, *Relation du voyage du Port Royal de l'Acadie* [1708]
    (Amsterdam, 1710), p. 133.
11 François-René de Chateaubriand, *Travels in America and Italy*
    (London, 1828), vol. II, pp. 149, 151.
12 Gordon M. Sayre, *Les Sauvages Américains: Representations of
    Native Americans in French and English Literature* (Chapel Hill, NC,
    1997), pp. 230–38.
13 Pierre François-Xavier de Charlevoix, *Journal of a Voyage to North
    America*, trans. Louise Phelps Kellogg (Chicago, IL, 1923), vol. II,
    p. 117.
14 Buffon, *Natural History*, vol. VI, pp. 287–8.
15 Ibid., vol. VII, p. 39.
16 Ibid., vol. VII, p. 48; vol. X, p. 22.
17 Peter C. Messer, 'Republican Animals: Politics, Science and the
    Birth of Ecology', *Journal for Eighteenth-century Studies*, XXXIII/4
    (2010), pp. 599–600.
18 Ibid., p. 608.
19 Charlevoix, *Journal of a Voyage*, vol. I, p. 139.
20 Chateaubriand, *Travels*, p. 151.
21 John D. Godman, *American Natural History* (Philadelphia, PA,
    1826), vol. II, pp. 34–5.

22 Jean de La Fontaine, 'The Two Rats, the Fox and the Egg', *The Original Fables of La Fontaine*, trans. Frederick Colin Tilney (London, 1913), pp. 81–2.

23 Ernest Menault, *The Intelligence of Animals, with Illustrative Anecdotes* (New York, 1869), p. 226.

24 Lewis H. Morgan, *The American Beaver and His Works* [1898] (Philadelphia, 1868), p. 191.

25 Ibid., p. 256.

26 Gould and Grant Gould, *Animal Architects*, pp. 268–9.

27 Bernard Rudofsky, *The Prodigious Builders* (New York, 1977), pp. 13, 59, 57.

5 ECOLOGIST

1 Grey Owl, *Pilgrims of the Wild* [1935] (Dundurn, 2010), p. 71.

2 George Simpson, *Fur Trade and Empire: George Simpson's Journal*, ed. Frederick Merk (Cambridge, MA, 1931), p. 14.

3 Quoted in Lorne Hammond, 'Marketing Wildlife: The Hudson's Bay Company and the Pacific Northwest, 1821–1849', *Forest and Conservation History*, XXXVII/1 (1993), p. 17.

4 Tina Loo, *States of Nature: Conserving Canada's Wildlife in the Twentieth Century* (Vancouver, 2006), p. 95–6.

5 Dolly Jørgensen, 'Hunters as Godfathers', dolly.jorgensenweb.net, 30 January 2013.

6 Dolly Jørgensen, 'Opening the Box', dolly.jorgensenweb.net, 10 November 2013.

7 Grey Owl, *Pilgrims*, p. 67.

8 Mike Hansell, *Animal Architecture* (Oxford, 2005), pp. 209–10.

9 Glynnis Hood, *The Beaver Manifesto* (Victoria, 2011), p. 52.

10 Elliott Coues, ed., *New Light on the Early History of the Greater Northwest: The Manuscripts of Alexander Henry and of David Thompson* (New York, 1897), vol. II, p. 724.

11 Rosalind Grace Morgan, 'Beaver Ecology/Beaver Mythology', PhD dissertation, University of Alberta, 1991.

12 Hood, *The Beaver Manifesto*, p. 115.

13 Steven Morris, 'First Wild Beavers to be Seen in England for Centuries to be Captured', *The Guardian*, 30 June 2014.

14 Senator Nancy C. Eaton, 'The Polar Bear', Senate of Canada, www.parl.gc.ca, 27 October 2011.

15 Tamsin McHahon, 'Ottawa Farmers Declare War on the Beaver', *National Post*, 31 October 2011.

16 Charles Choi, 'Tierra del Fuego: The Beavers Must Die', *Nature*, CCCCLIII/7198 (2008), p. 968.

17 Emma Marris, 'Goodbye Galapagos Goats', www.nature.com/nature, 27 January 2009.

Select Bibliography

Buffon, Comte de (Georges-Louis Leclerc), *Barr's Buffon: Buffon's Natural History* (London, 1797–1807)

Buyukmihci, Hope Sawyer, *Hour of the Beaver* (Chicago, IL, 1971)

Carlos, Ann M. and Frank D. Lewis, *Commerce by a Frozen Sea: Native Americans and the European Fur Trade* (Philadelphia, PA, 2010)

Coles, Bryony, *Beavers in Britain's Past* (Oxford, 2006)

Dent, Anthony, *Lost Beasts of Britain* (London, 1974)

Diamond, Reid, and Marnie Fleming, *Beaver Tales*, exh. cat., Oakville Galleries, Oakville, Ontario (Oakville, 2000)

Dolin, Eric Jay, *Fur, Fortune, and Empire: The Epic History of the Fur Trade in America* (New York, 2010)

Dugmore, A. Radclyffe, *The Romance of the Beaver* (Philadelphia, PA, 1914)

Gagnon, François-Marc, *Images du Castor Canadien xvie–xviiie siècles* (Quebec, 1994)

Gould, James L., and Carol Grant Gould, *Animal Architects: Building and the Evolution of Intelligence* (New York, 2007)

Hood, Glynnis, *The Beaver Manifesto* (Victoria, 2011)

Innis, Harold A., *The Fur Trade in Canada* (New Haven, CT, 1930)

Martin, Horace T., *Castorologia; or, The History and Traditions of the Canadian Beaver* (Montreal, 1892)

Mills, Enos A., *In Beaver World* (Boston, MA, 1913)

Morgan, Lewis H., *The American Beaver and His Works* (Philadelphia, PA, 1868)

Morgan, Rosalind Grace, 'Beaver Ecology/Beaver Mythology', PhD
     dissertation, University of Alberta, Edmonton, 1991
Müller-Schwarze, Dietland, *The Beaver: Its Life and Impact*, 2nd edn
     (Ithaca, NY, 2011)
Nadeau, Chantal, *Fur Nation: From the Beaver to Brigitte Bardot*
     (London, 2001)
Richards, Dorothy, and Hope Sawyer Buyukmihci, *Beaversprite:
     My Years Building an Animal Sanctuary* (San Francisco, CA, 1977)
Sandoz, Mari, *The Beaver Men: Spearheads of Empire* (New York, 1964)
Sayre, Gordon M., *Les Sauvages Américains: Representations of
     Native Americans in French and English Colonial Literature*
     (Chapel Hill, NC, 1997)

Associations and Websites

BEAVER DECEIVERS, INTERNATIONAL
www.beaverdeceivers.com
Beaver Deceiver™ inventor Skip Lisle's website.

BEAVER SOLUTIONS
www.beaversolutions.com
A beaver management service that specializes in resolving beaver-related flooding problems.

BEAVERS: WETLANDS AND WILDLIFE
www.beaversww.org
An educational non-profit organization focused on the environmental benefits of beaver wetlands and finding peaceful solutions to beaver–human conflicts.

BOB ARNEBECK'S BEAVERS
www.bobarnebeck.com
A comprehensive site discussing beaver behaviour and beaver lore.

SCOTTISH BEAVER TRIAL
www.scottishbeavers.org.uk
Official home of the Scottish Beaver Trial, the United Kingdom's first formal mammal reintroduction scheme.

SOUTHLAND BEAVER
www.southlandbeaver.blogspot.com
Duane Nash's blog about beavers, particularly those in southern
California.

UNEXPECTED WILDLIFE REFUGE
www.unexpectedwildliferefuge.org
A wildlife sanctuary started by Cavit and Hope Buyukmihci, founders
of the Beaver Defenders.

WORTH A DAM
www.martinezbeavers.org
A non-profit dedicated to inspiring and educating urban communities
on the benefits of co-existing with beavers.

Acknowledgements

Special thanks go to Jonathan Burt, Michael Leaman and everyone at Reaktion for their thoughtful contributions and assistance in the making of this book. For their valuable knowledge, insights and comments I would like to thank Joshua Samuels, Tina Loo, Dolly Jørgensen, Frank Narve Rosell, Natalia Rybczynski, Janet Yee and Skip Lisle. For their generosity with images, a special thank you goes to Swann Paradis, Michael LeValley, Ann Marie Stevenson, Sarah Pearson and Sam Alberti, Ginny A. Roth and Melanie Modlin, Marguerite Ragnow, Maura Doyle, Heidi Perryman, Peter Cornelissen, Simon Jones, Wendy Coburn and Christy Gast. And finally, a heartfelt thanks to all my family and friends who endured more beaver talk than is quite necessary, but most especially to Tobias Slezak, Judy Poliquin and the littlest beaver of all, Theodore Wren.

Photo Acknowledgements

Alexander E. MacDonald Canadiana Collection / Library and Archives Canada, Ottawa: p. 130; photo Isaac Applebaum: p. 117; photo Linda Armstrong / Shutterstock.com: p. 180; courtesy of Bayerische Staats-bibliothek, Munich: p. 26 (top); © Beaver Solutions LLC: p. 191; courtesy of Beavers: Wetlands & Wildlife: p. 177; photo Bildagentur Zoonar GmbH / Shutterstock.com: p. 148; The Bodleian Libraries, The University of Oxford: pp. 56, 63; photo Mickey Bohnacker: p. 104; British Library, London (photos © The British Library): pp. 55, 69; British Museum, London (photo © Trustees of the British Museum): pp. 20, 134, 181; photos © Trustees of the British Museum, London: pp. 33, 90, 101; photos Jessica Bushey: pp. 12, 124; photo camillareads.com: p. 100; from Lewis Carroll, *Alice's Adventures in Wonderland* (London, 1890): p. 106; from Moyse Charas, *Theriaque d'Andromachus* . . . (Paris, 1668): p. 72; photo Stephanie Coffman / Shutterstock.com: p. 157; photo Collection Estampes et illustrations anciennes, © Direction des Biblio-thèques, Université de Montréal, Québec, Canada: p. 87; collection of the New York Historical Society: p. 89; courtesy of the artist (Marianne Corless): p. 93; courtesy of Maura Doyle: p. 156; from Radclyffe Dugmore, *The Romance of the Beaver* (London, 1914): pp. 142, 146; from Arthur Charles Fox-Davies, *A Complete Guide to Heraldry* (London, 1909): p. 26 (foot); Frans Hals Museum, Haarlem: pp. 96, 97; photo Christy Gast: p. 196; from Christy Gast, *Castor Chef* (2014): p. 48; pro-duction still from Christy Gast, *Castorera, A Love Story* (2014): p. 199; German Historical Museum, Berlin: p. 100; photo Rosemary Gilliat Eaton / Library and Archives Canada, Ottawa: p. 143; from Jacques

Grasset de Saint-Sauveur, *Encyclopédie des voyages, contenant l'abrégé historique des moeurs, usages, habitudes domestiques . . . de tous les peuples . . .* (Paris, 1796): p. 87; photo Tom Haartsen: pp. 96, 97; from Elmo Heter, 'Transplanting Beavers by Airplane and Parachute', *Journal of Wildlife Management*, xiv/2 (April, 1950): p. 183; Hudson's Bay Company Archives, Archives of Manitoba, Winnipeg: pp. 166, 167; photo George Hunter / National Film Board of Canada (Photothèque / Library and Archives Canada, Ottawa): p. 84; Hunterian Museum, Royal College of Surgeons of England, London: p. 34; photo Rob Huntley / Shutterstock.com: p. 140; courtesy of the James Ford Bell Library, University of Minnesota, Minneapolis: p. 131; photos © Jamtlis Arkiv: pp. 154 (photo NTh 7513= Erik Brännholm), 169 (photo NTh 7504= Okänd), 170 (photo NTh 626= Nils Thomasson); photo Alan Jeffery / Shutterstock.com: p. 30; photo Catriona Jeffries: p. 116; photos © John Carter Brown Library, Providence, Rhode Island: pp. 75, 83, 138; photo Gail Johnson / Shutterstock.com: p. 47; photo Dolly Jørgensen: p. 165; photo Piotr Kamionka / Shutterstock.com: p. 49; photo Scott Karcich / Shutterstock.com: p. 8; photo Charles Knowles / Shutterstock.com: p. 163; photo LesPalenik / Shutterstock.com: p. 44; photo Efraim Lev and Zohar Amar, Wellcome Images: p. 58; photo Michael J. LeValley: p. 43; photo Libraries and Archives of Canada, Ottawa: pp. 78, 119, 149, 160, 172, 174, 176; Lovat Dickson Collection / Library and Archives Canada, Ottawa: p. 161; photo Bruce MacQueen / Shutterstock.com: p. 13; photo Mary Evans Picture Library: p. 136; photo Doug Meek / Shutterstock.com: p. 192; from Lewis Henry Morgan, *The American Beaver* (Philadelphia, PA, 1868): pp. 21, 122, 151, 153; from Cromwell Mortimer, 'The Anatomy of a *Female Beaver*, and an Account of *Castor* found in her', *Philosophical Transactions*, xxxviii (1753): p. 30; photo National Library of Medicine, Bethesda, Maryland: p. 34; National Portrait Gallery, London (photos © National Portrait Gallery): pp. 80, 94, 99; courtesy of Oakville Galleries, Oakville, Ontario: p. 117; photo Osher Map Library, University of Southern Maine, Portland: p. 127; photo Michael Padwee, tilesinnewyork.blogspot.com: p. 108; reproduced courtesy of Parks Canada: p. 175; image courtesy of Peel's Prairie Provinces (peel.library.ualberta.ca), a digital initiative of the University of Alberta Libraries, Edmonton, Alberta: p. 114; from Claude Perrault, *Description anatomique d'un cameleon, d'un castor, d'un dromadaire, d'u ours et d'une gazelle* (Paris, 1669): p. 33; Peter Winkworth Collection of Canadiana / Library and Archives Canada, Ottawa: pp. 19, 182; from Philippe de Thaon's *Bestiare*: p. 27; photo Photopictures / Shutterstock.com: p. 194; from Matthaeus Platearius, *The Book of Simple Medicines*: p. 23; from Noël Antoine Pluche, *Spectacle de la Nature; or, Nature Display'd . . .* (London, 1763): p. 136; photos private collections: pp. 10, 41, 54; photo Dan H Ralston / u.s. Fish and Wildlife Service: p. 105; from Frank Rosell and Lixing Sun, 'Use of Anal Gland Secretion to Distinguish the Two Beaver Species *Castor canadensis* and *C. fiber*', *Wildlife Biology*, v/1 (1999): p. 77; courtesy of the Royal Library Denmark, Copenhagen: p. 27; Russian National Library, Leningrad: p. 23; courtesy of the artist (Kari Rust): p. 120; photo © St Gallen, Stiftsbibliothek: p. 24 (foot); photo Tobias Slezak: p. 188; photo courtesy of Special Collections, University of Houston Libraries: p. 60; photo courtesy of Spencer Collection, The New York Public Library, Astor, Lenox, and Tilden Foundations: p. 64; photo SuperStock: p. 23; courtesy of theprintcollector.com: pp. 16, 36, 37, 38, 65 (foot); from Edward Topsell, *The History of Four-footed Beasts and Serpents* (London, 1658): p. 60; courtesy of ubc Museum of Anthropology, Vancouver, Canada: pp. 12, 124; photo courtesy of Unexpected Wildlife Refuge: p. 197; photo Jeremy Usher-Smith, Royal Zoological Society Scotland: p. 185; photo Karen Wolf: p. 65 (top); courtesy of Worth A Dam and Gianna of Las Juntas Elementary School third grade, Martinez, California: p. 190; courtesy of the artist (Jin-me Yoon): p. 93; photo Karim Zouak: p. 135.

Index